Westbury, Marcus
Creating Cities
ISBN: 978-0-9925687-4-0

Cover by Damien Frost
Edited by Jessica Friedmann
Typesetting and layout by Sarah Bunting
Project support by Marnie Kay

Some material reproduced with the permission of the authors/owners as acknowledged on pp.188-191

First published August 2015 by Niche Press
Melbourne, Australia. (03) 9939 1229
www.nichepress.com.au michael@nichepress.com.au

Creating Cities is a Marcus Westbury project
www.creatingcities.net marcus@marcuswestbury.net

A CIP catalogue record for this book is available from the National Library of Australia.

Marcus Westbury—

CREATING CITIES

For Narinda, Louin and Otto.

CONTENTS

Preface—

A SIGN ON A HILL

In a forgotten few months in the 1960s, my grandfather Bert Webber built a sign.

A few hundred metres up the road from the weatherboard cottage where my mother grew up there is a park. It was cobbled together from the remains of the quarry out of which they had once built Newcastle's iconic breakwater, one of the city's major water reservoirs, and a firing range.

Braye Park hill has always felt a little like an afterthought. Despite commanding views back over the city of Newcastle and out to the Pacific Ocean, the park has always been an orphaned space. My guess is that it became a park largely because there wasn't much else you could do with it. By the 1960s it was backed onto by housing developments, a nursing home, and the Mater Hospital, where I was born.

It was a sprawling, unwieldy site, with a wooden fort I

remember exploring with my grandmother as a kid. Others might remember it better as one of Newcastle's more infamous gay beats. Regardless of your reason to go, it was never a particularly easy place to find your way towards. To drive up there from the main road you needed to take a barely marked turn up a steep and nondescript hill at a service building that looked to all the world like a 1950s toilet block.

For reasons unknown, Granda took it upon himself to fix that aspect of it. He built a sign in his back shed—a metal circle with several flat wooden crosspieces, almost certainly inspired by something in one of his cherished *Popular Mechanics* encyclopaedias. To this day I've never really known how, or why, or exactly when. I don't know who his co-conspirators were, or whether he acted alone.

As a boy, the 'Braye Park' sign with its simple lettering in what looks like a cross-section of an old Coopers barrel was bigger than I was. It probably still is. I have a mental picture of Granda, with a begged or borrowed trailer, towing it up the hill behind his vintage Holden, and with the help of a few of his mates cementing it firmly into place.

It's family mythology, one of those stories that has probably gotten better every time it has been told. The sign, though, is still there. It survived a long period of disrepair in my teenage years, when I figured it would soon be gone for good. These days it has been restored, and is minimally maintained. It's a minor local icon.

I like it. It's an idiosyncratic oddity in a sea of suburban sameness. Over the years it has gradually gotten more and more out of context with the uniform, bureaucratic designed-by-committee signs and symbols that adorn most other public parks.

Like most things that form the texture and detail of a city, I suspect most people never give it a second glance. But since I was a boy, every time I've passed I've felt a small ripple of pride.

My grandfather was a child of the Great Depression and the Second World War. He was a practical and pragmatic man, with little time for pretensions. He died when I was seven or eight. I remember him in images, tinkering in his shed. His world-worn and weathered hands. Him showering us with presents when he won a bet on the trifecta, and passionately following Wests Newcastle in the local rugby league.

I'm not sure he'd see the lineage between the sign he raised on that hill those many decades ago and the ideas outlined in this book. But that sign has always animated me. It has given me a sense of place, of continuity and connection. It has given me something else: an idea planted in the concrete up there. The idea that you could *do* that. That a community is built *up* by the thousands of actions from hundreds of individuals and their collaborations, and not *down* from the whims of the few. A recurring reminder that a community is something you make and remake through your actions.

Of course, Bert's burst of hands-on civic self-improvement came a few generations ago. Bert was forged in a working-class steel town, a child of lean and rough times where resilient resourcefulness was a survival skill and a necessity. He lived through a depression and the Second World War. When the war ended, his generation set about building a new dream.

Australian suburbs were built on that generation's initiative and resourcefulness. You could see it in the bowling clubs and the sporting facilities, the parks and the playgrounds, and a whole range of civic infrastructure. In leaner times much of it was built on a partnership between pooled funds and community fundraising. It was built by the effort, sweat and skills of many people, cheap—often public—lands and the sense that no frills community-built facilities were more than enough.

The suburbs of my childhood were dotted with that legacy. But somewhere between Bert's generation and mine—often, for the better—things stopped working like that. The no-frills community-built infrastructure of the post-war years gradually gave way. Some of it disappeared through age and obsolescence. The women and men who had built and maintained it moved and passed on.

Places like the Wests Leagues Club became formalised, consolidated and grew bigger. Cars meant that we could make do with fewer, bigger, and often better facilities. Other places fell under the spell of corporate management, growth targets, and poker machines. They become more and more detached from the communities that had once built them.

I'm not sure exactly *when* it happened, but somewhere along the line between my parents' generation and my own, we forgot that it could work like it did in Bert's time. Public space became more regulated, and the once-simple intersection between individual and community action, civic improvement and control became more and more complex.

Cities became expensive, privatised, professionalised and bureaucratised. Infrastructure became the job of master planners and middle managers. Societies became more individualistic, more competitive, and more unequal. People got busy. They ran out of time for such things.

By the time I came of age, the idea that an individual could build something in their shed and place it permanently on public lands was almost unthinkable. Doing it yourself was not an easy option. You'd need a ten-million-dollar insurance policy. There were a dozen very well-intentioned sets of city-wide design guidelines. An old man lashing a massive sign to his car would probably violate at least half a dozen traffic ordinances and Occupational Health and Safety rules.

Bert was a patient man but not one for risk reviews, planning and objection processes. Such things are for people who work with their heads, not their hands. For masters of process, not enthusiastic punters. For those with capital, not old craftsmen with concrete and a car.

We mostly didn't notice—for the most part because this was a good thing. Our cities got safer and cleaner, neater and more orderly, tamer and more professionally managed than they have ever been. Perhaps we simply haven't needed the Bert Webbers of the world. The system caught such needs and addressed them.

But along the way we lost something. Something that in an era of new challenges, new crises, and new opportunities has become more important and more apparent. Our cities had become less participatory, less open and less adaptive. Of course there have still been shining examples of communities initiating their own projects, but these are rarer and the process much harder than it had been.

We gained something, but we lost something. Rethinking that balance between professionalisation and participation, between enthusiasm and control, between risk and regulation has led me to this book.

Creating Cities is the result of nearly two decades of observing, prodding, banging my head against, untangling and hacking, defeating and being defeated by the broken systems of our cities. It is a story that begins in the shadow of Braye Park Hill but it is one that ripples across hundreds, if not thousands, of communities around the world.

It is the story of changing cities and changing opportunities; of an unlikely transformation in Newcastle that has in turn fed and fed off many others across Australia and around the world. It is the story of what that transformation was; the accumulation of accidents and opportunities that catalysed it and how it happened. More importantly it is the story of *why*.

I'm not an architect, a town planner or an economist. I am Bert Webber's grandson. I have only studied cities through trial and error. I have been a festival director, TV presenter and service station attendant; I have met hundreds, if not thousands, of people with projects and initiatives, imagination and ideas. I have seen what happened when they came up against the systems of our modern cities and realised those systems were squandering their enthusiasm.

I am the product of my own failed projects and unrealised dreams. These, and the odd successful one in between, have taught me much about how cities work or fail to at the practical level—at the smallest of scales. The more I tried and the more I failed, the more I learned, and the more I became sidetracked and obsessed not by the usual questions of how cities are built, but by often unspoken ones of how cities behave.

What grips me is how places enable or thwart people with initiative, and how people who simply aspire to try ideas or make a contribution through their actions *are* or *are not* able to do so. I gradually began to realise just how many towns, cities and communities—particularly those like Newcastle that aren't the shining centres of global capital—desperately need them to.

This book is a gentle provocation to many professions, business, and political leaders left and right. It argues that we are doing it wrong a lot of the time. Doing it as we feel we always have done it. Doing it as our spreadsheets, our fractured, professionalised and detached plans and strategies tell us we should do it. Yet, when we look up, the world is behaving differently.

It is changing dramatically, but in some respects it is bringing us back full circle. Changing cultural, technological, economic and social dynamics are returning us to a set of ideas and expectations that my grandfather's generation could not afford to not understand.

Our places are not merely physical spaces. They are not purely architectures and objects. They are collections of forces, of motivations and opportunities. Too often passions and possibilities are neutered by mechanical, unintentional, even mundane trivialities.

Our cities aren't simply grand projects and megavisions; they are constellations of small acts and activities. They are the seeding ground for unlikely possibilities and tiny revolutions. They are interconnected with and enabled by much larger forces of information and economics that are rewriting communities and possibilities across the globe.

My experiences have taught me that cities can become unintentionally, banally, disinterestedly dysfunctional. They often don't even realise that they are doing it. I've seen echoes of that problem in cities, towns, communities and suburbs around the world: across the USA, Canada, New Zealand, England, Scotland, Portugal, China, Columbia, Chile and Italy.

I have also seen the beginning of a change. New opportunities and possibilities have emerged. Subtle, invisible, but massive changes in the world have created possibilities that were not available only a handful of years ago. The same forces that have seen retail, manufacturing and commercial economies retreat from the places in which they once thrived are also bringing with them new and previously unimagined possibilities.

The resourceful, community minded, do-it-yourself ethos of my grandfather's generation has begun to meet the connectedness, technology and possibilities of today. *Popular Mechanics* has given way to global communities, blogs, movements, markets and networks of inspiration that prime people to realise invisible possibilities lurking just beneath the surface. Yet most places don't quite seem to know how to nurture them yet.

If nothing else, *Creating Cities* is a plea to rediscover the possibilities of people in a world designed around capital. It is an argument to recognise that the imagination, the sweat, the enthusiasm, and the efforts of its people are the greatest resource that any place has as its disposal. Harnessing this enthusiasm does not merely provide tangible and measurable benefits, but something intangible and invaluable: community, connection and cohesiveness.

There are great possibilities lying latent in most communities. To realise them requires a new understanding of how cities work, what drives them, and how they might evolve. They involve thinking about how people want and need their places to behave in the 21st Century, and creating the context, the conditions and the climate to meet them there.

Part One—

BROKEN CITIES

Chapter One—

A NEWCASTLE STORY

For decades, Newcastle was the BHP Steelworks. We grew up in its shadow. The night sky was lit by the flames of blast furnaces, and the city set its rhythms to its changes of shifts. In nearby suburbs, mothers and grandmothers played washing-line roulette around its belching smoke and changes of wind direction. It was a city of a few hundred thousand people, and at its peak, a tenth or more of the Novocastrian workforce was employed in the steelworks. The whole city was directly and indirectly dependent on it.

I'm not sure that anyone saw what was coming. In images and advertisements of Newcastle in the 1970s and early '80s, there is a naivety and little hint of foreboding. Newcastle had prospered through labour-intensive, protected, and globally exposed industries from steel-making to textiles, ship-building and shipping. These jobs were soon to be automated, off-shored, outsourced, containerised, and traded away. It was a fate that befell dozens, if not hundreds, of similar cities around the Western world.

Back then, my grandmother would dress us up to go shopping in town. Local television and radio advertising created household names out of local retailers who were peppered among national chains and sold global brands. The city centre was busy, vibrant and prosperous.

The tram network from which Newcastle got the logic of its layout had gone before I was born, but for a while it seemed not to matter. Cars, trains, and buses still brought people in their thousands. They came, as we did, from the suburbs, and from across the Hunter Valley. They shopped in Newcastle's grand department stores and specialty shops. They drank and met in its dozens of pubs and nightclubs and worked by day in busy offices. Even as the first suburban supermarkets were beginning to morph into shopping centres, none had the glamour or the destination appeal of a day out in 'town'.

The Newcastle of my youth had a gritty working-class pride. It was rough 'round the edges, but eclectic if you knew where to look. It had undercurrents and subcultures. It occasionally erupted. It was the scene for one Australia's most infamous urban riots—sparked by the clumsy handling of the closure of the iconic Star Hotel, but reflecting deeper tensions that lingered below the surface. It was a place of labour and unions, where The Workers Club was literally and metaphorically central to many social lives.

It was progressive and left-of-centre. It was the first large Australian city to have a female mayor, but looking back, it was a blokey and male-dominated culture. In the '70s the eponymous 'Newcastle Song' was a national hit that popularised the city as a town of mostly harmless gormless men who yelled woeful pickup lines at women from cars. It was as true as any stereotype, but it wasn't always gormless and it wasn't always harmless. Not much changed for the next few decades. As a teenage boy, without particularly knowing why, my friends and I did the same for a while.

By the '80s and '90s, even as the rest of Australia had begun to change, Newcastle was disproportionately white and working-class. It had buried its Awabakal and Woromi history under the heavy hand of early European settlement. Southern European migrants had come to work in the steelworks in the '50s, but latter waves of Asian migrants had largely passed the city by. It was less that they weren't welcome; rather that by then, migrants sought out places upon which the sun was rising, not setting.

My own family's fortunes tracked those of the city that we lived in. My father sold used cars in Mayfield, the same suburb as the steelworks. In the 1980s, the first round of BHP lay-offs destroyed his business and my parents' marriage. It was the beginning of a chain of events that eventually destroyed them both. He left town and gradually drifted from reality.

My mother stumbled on, but neither she nor Newcastle could catch a break. In 1989 an earthquake—at the time the most expensive natural disaster in Australia's history—broke the back not just of the city, but of us. My mother worked in a health food store in the city. It was one of dozens of inner city businesses that never opened again.

By the time I left high school and moved out of home in the early 1990s, the city's decline was unavoidable. After several rounds of layoffs at BHP, an earthquake, the loss of major industries like shipbuilding, and recessions large and small, Newcastle was visibly struggling.

The tallest building in the city sat vacant and derelict for decades. Unemployment in the city peaked in the mid-teens. Youth unemployment—for my friends and my peers—was more than 40%. Everyone I knew was either studying or unemployed. When I was twenty almost no one I knew had a job. Very few even had the vaguest prospect of one.

The earthquake had been a tipping point. It damaged or destroyed hundreds of major buildings and thousands of minor ones. The Workers Club collapsed, killing nine people. The entire city centre was cordoned off by the army for weeks, which finally turned the slow flight of retail and commercial business to the suburbs into a wave.

The absence of government—Newcastle at the time was the largest city in Australia that wasn't a state or territory capital—meant that there was little to hold the centre together. As the insurance money and the major projects wore off, Newcastle gradually drifted into deterioration on a scale with few parallels in any other major Australian city.

Politics and politicians were disinterested. The local seats were so safe for the Labor Party that they saw no point in defending them, and the conservative parties saw no prospect of winning them. By the time the steelworks finally closed in 1999, the damage had largely been done.

As a 19- or 20-year-old, you take such things for granted. It is what it is. Newcastle's youth culture was part DIY, part drugs, part activism and part nihilism. We lost friends and family to drugs, to excess, to despair, to suicide and stupidity. But there were worse places to be poor and unemployed. You could live in a share-house in an old terrace a few hundred metres from one of Australia's most beautiful beaches.

Despite its challenges it was always a city with a sense of self-reliance and civic pride. There were always things to get involved in; creative and community projects, protests and provocations, parties and events. It was a place and a time of cheap fun, cheap cask wine, and resilient self-entertainment—but all with a lingering sense that there may not be a tomorrow.

As the industries closed and shut up shop, they revealed something that in all my years of growing up there I'd somehow never noticed. As they demolished and cleaned up the city centre power station, as the working docks and rail-yards became parklands, as the smoke and industrial haze receded, they revealed a city that was naturally and architecturally beautiful. This was an old city sitting on a peninsula crowned by a commanding cliff face, looking out onto the Pacific Ocean. Crystal blue water and golden beaches lined one side, and a working harbour with a constant procession of coal ships animated the other.

Newcastle was an accidental time capsule. It had begun as a punitive penal colony for the worst of the worst. By the turn of the millennium it had one of the largest cluster of intact early European buildings in Australia. Rather than overwriting its history as most Australian cities had done, it had grown linearly, out along the tram tracks towards the pit towns that would eventually become its suburbs.

You could walk from the Art Deco ocean baths and the beaches at one end, along a decaying Hunter Street towards the west, and journey through a history of Australian architecture. Starting from the convict settlement, and winding through the retail and commercial buildings of the late 19th and early 20th Century, you arrived in a once-confident civic core with its Spanish Baroque Town Hall and Georgian Revival Civic Theatre. These iconic buildings had been built with confidence as the city boomed with the coming of the steelworks in the 1920s.

Growing up, I don't remember anyone describing Newcastle as *beautiful*. It didn't help that Sydney, the next city along, is one of the most spectacularly beautiful in the world. You begin with a chip on your shoulder when you're the unfortunate, undernourished sibling of a supermodel. While no match for Sydney's spectacular harbour, Newcastle still has many of its charms and few of its pretensions. Decades of decline and neglect have preserved layers of history and character in Newcastle that shonky developers and short-term dollars made disappear in Sydney.

In Newcastle I found a community and an opportunity. 'Amusing ourselves' grew into our own arts and community organisation. My obsessions grew into a festival that in turn grew into the city's largest annual tourism event and one of the largest arts and DIY media events in Australia. None of it grew into a living.

I never really wanted to leave Newcastle. You are meant to want to escape your hometown, but if that was ever my ambition, it was fleeting. Eventually, it was the reality of the unemployment rate and the need to make a living that took me to Sydney. I discovered that people in other cities would pay you to do the kinds of events and projects that we were doing in Newcastle for free.

Between jobs I moved back, but I ultimately landed in

Melbourne where I fell in love, got married, and eventually had two children. They say you should never look back—but I never stopped looking.

Chapter Two—

EXPLORATIONS IN EMPTINESS

In late 2007 and early 2008, I found myself walking Hunter and King Streets, the two main streets of Newcastle, and the smaller streets that connected them. I was seeing them afresh—looking at parts of them up close for the first time in the best part of a decade. I spent two days peering in windows, noting down vacancies, taking camera-phone photographs and notes about particular buildings and likely spaces.

I knew Newcastle had seen better days, but what I saw on that weekend was confronting and depressing. Empty buildings featured faded 'For Lease' signs. Several still had real estate agent contact details featuring an area code that Newcastle had phased out in 1997.

I was there because I was at a loose end. I was between jobs, technically unemployed again but not as desperate as I had been a decade earlier. I had some money in the bank and some time on my hands. I'd been living in Melbourne for five years but was toying with the idea of heading home to Newcastle to start a small bar, gallery and performance space.

It is a sidenote to this story that the Australian state of New South Wales, where Newcastle and Sydney are located, had long had the world's worst liquor licensing regime outside of Saudi Arabia. Cronyism, lobbying, and quirks of history had meant that for decades, liquor licenses had come bound up with the right to run slot machines.

It is a case study in extreme barriers to entry, patronage, protectionism, and insulating existing entrants from innovation or competition that is worthy of a book in and of itself. The state only offered a limited number of licenses and as a result, anyone wanting to set up a bar had needed millions of dollars to buy out an existing license and was lumbered with the expectation (and economics) of running a gambling den.

In the mid 2000s that changed, as the result of considerable community pressure. Small bar licenses were introduced and under the new system, I suddenly had the opportunity to realise a long-held dream. Initially it wasn't much more than a thought bubble—an idea worth investigating. I bought myself a copy *Running a Bar for Dummies* and broadly familiarised myself with the relevant legislation.

I'd been peripherally involved in the licensing reform campaign and was able to pick the brains of some of the people involved. I convinced myself that Newcastle would embrace a more diverse drinking, dining, music, art and entertainment scene, and hopped on a plane for the hour-and-a half flight from Melbourne to Newcastle to do a bit of on-the-ground leg-work.

What followed was not the first (and hopefully not the last) time in my life that an enthusiastic interest in one idea has been derailed by the discovery of another.

Newcastle was dying. I thought I had no illusions, but everywhere I looked the rot was worse than I remembered. Streets that in my memories were vibrant, active, and filled with family and friends had fallen into disrepair and despair. Entire blocks were dominated by buildings that had been boarded up, gutted, and destroyed. As you entered the city from the west, there was a derelict hotel on one side and dust gathering on the empty glass of a new building that had never had a tenant opposite it.

Up near the beach, Newcastle's grandest building, the 1903-built Post Office with its domes, arches, and sandstone columns sat empty, tagged and fenced off. A few blocks away, the Victoria Theatre, the second-oldest theatre in Australia, sat broken and lifeless. The shop that had once occupied its foyer was abandoned. Windows were broken, seemingly inviting further decay.

The mall in between was more than half-empty. A contagious blight of abandoned spaces and boarded up windows had spread to the point where it had a toehold on almost every block. It was worse than I had remembered, worse than I thought it could ever become. The city felt like it was not merely slipping, but accelerating into decay.

On that walk I counted a hundred and thirty empty buildings. Mostly shops, but a few that were obviously offices and commercial buildings as well. I later realised that I'd missed many of them. For my small bar idea, it didn't particularly deter me. I noted down a few buildings that were likely candidates and identified a few promising areas or precincts where my little bar idea might take root.

Given the massive number of vacancies, I was under the naive assumption that there would be plenty to choose from. It should, after all, be a renter's market. I took my notes and my photographs, headed back home to Melbourne, and began to chase up the property agents.

Then things got weird. Over several months I contacted thirteen separate commercial real estate agents. I gave them a price range, one that seemed reasonable given advertised rates for some less suitable commercial properties, and generous given the state of the town; some thoughts on preferred but flexible locations, specific indications of what I was looking for and multiple contact details.

I said I was willing to pay for some modest capital improvements. I offered to fly to Newcastle from Melbourne to inspect any properties that might be likely candidates. My initial fear was that I might well be run off my feet with phone calls and offers.

I needn't have worried. As I wrote in my blog at the time, my initial inquiries via email were a total failure. The total number of properties I was encouraged to look at was nil. The total number of phone calls received was nil. The total number of, "Thanks, but we don't have anything for you at the moment" emails was nil. Indeed, the total amount of communication from anyone in the Newcastle real estate industry was...nothing.

Picking up the phone to enquire about specific properties didn't actually help much either. Many of the agents' contact details I'd noted from windows were well out of date. They no longer handled the property. The owner who had engaged them no longer owned it or couldn't be contacted.

Many were not, in any serious sense, on the market at all. Some owners were still holding out for rents that were unrealistic, or for potential tenants to return who hadn't been seen for years. Agents were uninterested. A lot of property in Newcastle was actually owned by people who, despite the proliferation of 'For Lease' signs, weren't even going through the motions of marketing them. More often than not, no one returned the calls.

There was also a failure of imagination. At one point I turned my attention to a particular building, one that I knew well and that a friend's family had once operated a business from. Despite the building being on the market, available, seemingly in the right price range and seemingly suitable for the purpose, the agent simply couldn't be convinced to show it to me.

The agent saw his role, apparently, not just as being a broker but also as an authority on what was and wasn't a viable business model. He kept asking me what other businesses in the area were like my small bar. I frustratedly attempted to explain that changes to the law had meant that there couldn't possibly be any precedents. *You should come to Melbourne,* I explained, *there's lots of small bars down here.*

As we talked, it became increasingly clear that if he didn't get it, he wasn't interested. He had no reference points. He had no experience of or interest in the ideas I proposed. He felt no need to go through the motions of indulging me in a discussion about the price or particularities of an untested idea that he didn't understand and wasn't personally convinced by.

Perhaps that's a strategy with some logic to it in a successful area. Actually it probably isn't. But in an area where most of the existing businesses are closed or closing, this approach seemed almost painfully stupid. By definition the things most likely to succeed are the things no one has tried yet. Surely an untested approach—and lots of them—was exactly what the area needed more of... and urgently?

Something more substantial was wrong here. I lost sight of my original purpose—starting that bar is still on the long list of unrealised dreams—and became more and more intrigued as to why the market and the owners weren't behaving the way Economics 101 told me they should.

An oversupply of properties should have led to a drop in the market price. So many sellers and so few buyers in the market should have meant that agents and owners were falling over themselves for my business. But the response to my approaches was indifference and lack of interest.

It was a diagnosis out of kilter with the debate that the city was having at the time. The debates in local papers or in political circles had always begun from the premise that the reason the city was failing was due to a lack of interest and investment. No one wanted to do anything there. But as I had directly experienced, this wasn't always true. What if the problem was more complex? What if the problem was not that no one wanted to do anything but that those who wanted to, for whatever reasons, couldn't?

The problem for me was not entirely new. My friends and I had experienced similar issues ten or fifteen years earlier, when the city was nowhere near as far into its downward spiral. When we were twenty-somethings, my talented but almost universally undercapitalised friends and colleagues had a stream of ideas for projects and businesses from cafés, shops, studios and galleries and various other marginal propositions.

As we left university or entered the workforce with no realistic possibilities of finding a job, so many of us were, initially at least, attracted by the idea that we would make our own work. That we could start our own businesses, or at least make our own fun. But we always hit road-blocks of the bureaucratic and practical kind.

When we did actually manage to find a place, we used it to establish a community organisation with pooled unemployment loans founded in an old warehouse. It is still going strong in another location to this day.

When I was younger, I had put a lot of these problems down to inexperience. The city's establishment was probably right to be wary of a bunch of pretty rough-and-ready young guys with ill-defined ambitions, suspicious haircuts and questionable capacity. But in the years since, Newcastle had been going backwards, deteriorating and seemingly getting more desperate while my own level of experience had increased dramatically.

Here I was in my mid-thirties, established, financially capable, confident in my own abilities. I felt like I was back at square one, incapable of getting most real estate agents to return my call. When they did, they were overtly treating me like some kind of idiot because I wanted to do something different.

I wasn't alone. As I incredulously recounted my experiences to anyone who would listen and wrote about them on my blog, it became obvious that my experience wasn't an aberration. It turned out that Newcastle was full of similar stories. Shops that never opened. Offices that never existed. Galleries and studios that ended up elsewhere.

Over beers and coffees, in phone calls and emails, a pattern started to form. The people being shut out were people with ideas but little access to capital, networks, or professional expertise. Their ideas and efforts—whether they were good, bad or indifferent—were never given much of a chance. The system was, in effect, designed all wrong for their needs. A city in desperate need of imagination, effort, and ideas had inadvertently created a whole series of barriers that made it unlikely, if not impossible, for people to try them there.

The city had changed a lot since I was younger. But perhaps the biggest change that had taken place over the last fifteen years was in me. Once I may well have been inclined to tilt at the problems by getting angry with the agents and the owners. I thought about it. I registered the domain name stoptherot.org and briefly contemplated an angry campaign of plastering empty shop windows with protest signs, writing ranty op-eds against stupid landowners, and picketing real estate agents.

Fortunately the 2008 version was more patient and a little luckier. I now found the problem to be compelling. I was at a loose end, I had time on my hands, and I needed a new obsession. It was a dynamic that needed pragmatism more than protest. I gradually got sucked into asking why the city wasn't working for people like us, and how it might be made to work. Something systemic was wrong here, and I turned my attention to trying to figure out what that was.

Chapter Three—

PROBLEMS OF PROPERTY

At face value none of it made sense. Why, when there were so many empty spaces, were so few landlords or real estate agents interested in filling them? It was a problem that had become acute in Newcastle but was by no means unique to it. Some of the dynamics were peculiarly local, but most were at least echoed in other places. All are worthy of at least some explanation.

To begin with, many owners weren't actually trying to rent their properties—certainly not for anything like what the market would pay. Some were nothing but speculators. Many more were genuine investors and developers, with little reason to do anything and lots of reasons not to. The thoughtless and heartless speculator is a stereotype, but like many stereotypes it is sometimes true. But if that was the only problem, this story would have stopped there.

Many had acquired their land cheap as the city had bottomed

out. It cost little to hold onto, and these buyers figured they would make more money by selling it one day than they could gain from the hassle of using it at the time. Some properties were being land-banked. While the short-term rent value was almost nothing, the long-term prospects of what the owner anticipated would be a prime site—once time, the government, or someone else had done the hard work and made the city attractive to live in—could be substantial.

This strategy had been exacerbated by a range of policy decisions or non-decisions. In recognition of the need for long-term changes in the city, the city had relaxed development conditions. They wanted to encourage residents in the city. Height restrictions had been lifted in key parts of town, and the city was actively encouraging the development of new residential apartments.

It created a dynamic that was ripe for speculation—a classic law of unintended consequences that meant the fading commercial centre of Newcastle had become far more valuable for what it *could be* than what it *was*. The really valuable transformation would mostly mean rebuilding. Some sites were moving, but across the city the market wasn't ready yet. Absorbing the volume of apartments that could potentially be permitted would take decades.

The problem wasn't just speculation. There were real problems involved in doing *anything*. While building high was permitted, it was also complicated. Newcastle was literally undermined by a web of poorly documented coal-mining tunnels from the convict era. There are stories—potentially apocryphal—of developers almost literally pouring money down seemingly endless holes in an attempt to grout their sites and stabilise their footings.

Those were problems for the future though. In the interim there were few incentives for activity and many incentives for sitting tight. Big structural and infrastructural decisions were always just over the horizon. There was an endless debate about the train line that ran through the city. Whether you personally favoured keeping it, removing it, burying it, beautifying it, elevating it or replacing it with light rail, the debate itself was a symptom of the city's paralysis. The argument had been going on so long that there was almost certainly an Awabakal word for it.

For whatever reason, the issue had defied definitive resolution. It was one of many big projects that were on-again and off-again. The powerful signal to individual property owners in the uncertainty seemed to be, *Wait*. Even the most civic-minded of owners were unsure if their property might be sold or redeveloped next year or ten years from now. Something was always about to happen but never quite did. Conventional uses and leases in the interim simply threatened to introduce unnecessary hassle for comparatively little return.

Then there was the logic of tax and financing arrangements. In some cases, the owners of property were in no position to rent the properties even if they wanted to. For artificial reasons many properties had a nominal (but in practice unrealistic) rate below which the rent could not fall.

As best as I could understand it, some owners were highly leveraged. They'd borrowed against the property in an environment where valuations and lease values were linked. They couldn't lease them for less than they were supposed to be worth. To do so would risk writing down the value of the asset and, in extreme cases, risk insolvency if the bank decided to write the value down proportionally.

Better to maintain the fiction that the building was temporarily empty at a high potential rent than to admit it could only be occupied at a low one. The small returns from rent weren't worth opening up that risk.

Behind the opaque walls of the individuals, companies, and trusts that owned the properties there were also, in many cases, a lot of very specific reasons for not doing much. In some circumstances, properties were worth as much if not more as a tax loss than as a going concern. Writing off the losses on a property might actually be the most productive thing an owner could do with it.

Against these big structural challenges there were also some decidedly human ones. Families, with all the politics they involve. Cousins who had inherited a property from their grandfather but didn't talk to each other. Individuals with idiosyncrasies, agendas and vendettas. Owners too old and frail to do anything much; trusts, partnerships or structures of convenience designed by dealmakers who had long cut and run.

Too often properties were owned by dysfunctional entities. Some were designed with a view to tax minimisation, or to bundle up the ownership into units that small investors could buy into. They had no real management and little direction. It was no one's job to think strategically. Sometimes a property was handed to an agent in the hope that they could figure it out, and other times properties were effectively left unmanaged in any practical sense.

Beyond simply accepting a profitable offer, these structures were unable to make complex decisions—deadlocked by their own process. Even where one family member or stakeholder could think proactively, the ownership structures that they were working in meant they often couldn't implement ideas. In some cases they couldn't even communicate with their business partners, let alone bring them along with them.

I had once assumed that the properties must all be owned by shrewd and cunning speculators, with complex agendas and forward-looking plans. Often the reality was the opposite and much more mundane. Much of the property was owned by people who were literally amateurs: lawyers, doctors, accountants, small businesspeople, retirees and self-managed retirement funds.

They were people who had bought on impulse on a weekend visit a decade ago and barely thought about it since; certainly they had neither the time nor inclination nor need to think strategically about where they were heading with it. The property was fulfilling its purpose while literally doing nothing—showing up on the books as an asset, appreciating in capital value for the most part. Actually doing something with it was an unnecessary complication.

I became more sympathetic to the agents too. Because of the costs and incentives baked into the system, some deals literally weren't worth bothering with. The legal fees alone on a standard commercial contract are expensive. They make no sense if the paperwork costs more than an agent will earn from the deal. The way real estate agents are incentivised discourages them from looking at the *small* deals. They are paid on commissions, percentages that add up on large sales and long leases but pay little in the short term and on cheap sales.

Even where it was obvious to everyone that the area desperately needed activity, there was little guarantee that any agent leading such efforts would reap any benefits. High upfront costs—legal fees, bonds, and expected fit-outs—are the norm in the property industry, and yet were almost impossible to justify in such a depressed environment.

Embedded in all these concerns and complications was the overriding issue of cost. For many, the biggest costs were opportunity costs. Default leases were for periods of three, five, or ten years. It's a long time to forgo other options and other offers.

Against a backdrop that anticipates rapidly rising property values—something that held true in Australia for a very long time—the cost of locking the property away by leasing it can be considerable. A traditional business that needs certainty to invest capital but doesn't offer much in return can inadvertently prove very expensive if it means forgoing a sale or a development in coming years.

Finally, there were the burdens of regulation and the costs of actually doing anything. Newcastle's buildings were often old, often in a state of disrepair, and many had been empty long enough that they had missed several waves of changing safety standards and building codes. The uses for which they had been initially designed had passed. Changing uses was expensive.

It was particularly and disproportionately expensive if you wanted to do something small. A ten- or even hundred-thousand-dollar cost to comply with a regulation is small change to a multinational on a major development. It is an immovable barrier to entry for anyone without access to ten thousand dollars.

Too often, people had become stuck on slightly absurd regulatory requirements: the need to move a fire exit a few centimetres, to put in new doors or windows, to install a new elevator in an old building to meet an access code, to put in entirely new plumbing or kitchen or toilet facilities. Many of these things were perfectly reasonable in the context of a major renovation, but made a minor one impossible and uneconomic.

Just understanding these codes and obligations is a professional job. There is little latitude for amateurs—be they the owners or the potential users of vacant spaces. They literally cannot comprehend what they need to do without paying for advice they often can't afford. Many of these laws had exemptions, interpretations and exclusions that might provide a way around them, but to find them you needed advice, and to assert them you need advocacy. You usually needed to pay for it.

People were becoming stuck on simple questions. How do I even know if I need to submit a Development Application? What are the heritage guidelines? What do changing building codes and health and safety requirements mean if I reopen this place? What I am liable for, or will be negligent for not doing?

These should be simple questions, but in practice they weren't. Try calling the switchboard of your local government, actually finding the right person, and coming away with an answer that is both definitive and comprehensible. I never have.

It is an irony that laws I had once seen as limiting and regulating the behaviour of large developers were actually forcing the property industry into the hands of large developers. They were the only people who could afford to navigate their way through them. They had the expertise in-house or on a retainer. For the rest of us, the answers were often unknowable, and impossible for someone without access to a phalanx of lawyers, consultants, engineers and financiers to push through them.

Most people aren't trying to build ten-story apartment blocks, but the law and its processes don't always understand that. An adversarial system that assumes that they are and applies rules accordingly will most likely end up in producing nothing but ten-story apartment blocks. As the costs of the process become higher and the scale of needed returns grows higher with it, and the developments need to be bigger and therefore need to take longer, the risk of the project grows and so too must the scale of the reward.

There was something about scale and risk that wasn't being appreciated. Processes seemed to treat every development, every intervention, every project in the city as though they came with a similar level of risk—dangerous 'til proven otherwise. Yet, many things are not particularly risky and, as buildings literally crumbled and decayed around us, there was far less risk in action than in inaction.

The particular local problem was that Newcastle is a small-scale city. It is full of small shops and offices. The viability of those spaces for anything other than bulldozing in the short- to medium-term was dependent on their ability to adapt quickly and cheaply for whatever purpose they may serve. As I had begun to appreciate, most of the people who might be motivated to adapt them, while capable of actually doing it, lacked access to the required resources and expertise to get through the process.

The bigger picture in all this was bizarre. A city full of people desiring to do things, staring at a seeming surplus of space in which to do it. Dozens of property owners unintentionally driving down the value of their properties. Bankers concerned so much with the paper value of assets that they were running down the actual value. Perfectly legal and simple things that no one could confirm the legality and simplicity of.

Governments at all levels were obsessing over how they might revitalise the city while unintentionally and inadvertently making the problems worse by confused processes, deferred decisions, and making promises they could not keep. Everyone was acting in their own interest while the city as a whole was literally falling apart.

Demonising 'evil property developers' has become a kind of ritual sport in many of the circles I mix in. They are an easy target, and I have met some who genuinely deserve the scorn. But the reality was a lot more complex than the stereotypes let on. No doubt self-interest and disinterest were encouraging bad decisions, but so many were simply boxed in by the absence of practical alternatives.

Meeting with individual property owners, it was obvious that most were acting not necessarily out of greed but out of confusion and inertia. Some were as much the victim of a poorly designed system as anyone. For every big evil speculator there were half-a-dozen retirees or migrant families who had their life savings tied up in their properties.

I met the unfortunate and naive who had often bought off the plan on the basis of inflated projections of rental returns that had never materialised. I met the enthusiastic dreamers who had their own grand plan for their properties but, for whatever reason, couldn't get there yet—they would start next year, always next year. There were the people who were simply out of their depth and tangled up in bad advice. Many of them just had no money. They had spent money on improvement for tenants who had never come, or who had skipped out with years of unpaid rent remaining.

I had begun with the premature conclusion that it was the property owners that were destroying the city. Like most things, it wasn't as simple as that. In some cases that was true but most were as stuck as I was. They had few alternatives.

Chapter Four—

MASLOW'S HAMMER

Since I started down this path, my work with cities has brought me into contact with people from academia, government, development, urban planning, architecture, place-making and community development. Their profession is to understand places, communities, and their needs, and to design and implement responses to them.

From all of them I have gained knowledge and insights that go in-depth, and directions well beyond the limited scope of my own experience. I have sought opportunities to pick their brains, learn from their experiences, collaborate with them and harness their skills. But as I have done so, I've realised that the frames through which I see the city are very different from theirs.

It was never my job to think about failing cities or places or empty spaces. My interest was Newcastle. Without it, there is very little chance I would have given it a second thought. I was in some combination of the wrong place at the right time or vice versa. Yet sometimes, coming at a problem from a completely different angle can reveal possibilities that might otherwise remain unseen.

I was coming to the problem not as a planner or a politician—I had abandoned the idea that I was an investor. I wasn't a property owner or a bureaucrat with a budget. I came initially as a user with a problem. It helped that I came armed with experience, a community, expectations, and ingenuity gleaned from having worked in a very different context over many years.

In an age of specialisation, it is inevitable that we reach and rub up against the limitations of our own disciplines. We suffer from what psychologist Abraham Maslow described as the Law of the Instrument. Or, as I've colloquially understood it, the idea that if all you have is a hammer, everything looks like a nail.

Inevitably the problems you are confronted with—be they the challenges of empty buildings, failing retail, or the decline of towns or centres, blight, vandalism or decay—will be seen through the prism of your discipline. You attempt to apply the tools of your trade and your training to solving them.

When the problem stretches beyond what our tools are designed for we struggle with it. We will pass it up or down the chain. We will fail to see it or pretend not to see it. We will hit it harder and throw more resources at it. We will ignore it and hope it goes away.

I used to be a festival director. For the most part, that's my hammer. I'm a generalist, not a specialist. I sometimes write and present TV shows; I've worked midnight to dawn in a petrol station; I built websites, wrote a newspaper column for a year or two, got thrown out of a few university courses and have been occasionally employed as an off-and-on radio producer.

It is a practical experience, grounded in festivals, that taught me about what people want to do and how cities and places respond to them. The festivals I have started or worked on have largely been niche, young, enthusiastically-embraced and perpetually under-resourced.

With limited resources my best trick in making them work was a simple one: find people with talent, and become the means through which they are able to do things that they would not otherwise be able to do. Find people whose work you believe in and give them the tools, the promotion, the venues, the contexts, the networks and the audiences to try something they might not otherwise try.

The city has always been a platform for that. A city's empty spaces always looked less to me like intractable problems and more like wasted opportunities. They were assets, a raw material, and a resource. Wasted spaces were often more interesting than formal ones. Audiences liked to discover or rediscover them, and creative people enjoyed the challenge of reinventing and working with them. For a small period of time, even a handful of interesting things can dramatically change the trajectory of a place.

In 2007 and 2008 I knew something else. I knew a community of makers and creators. I had been working with them, watching their rise, talking, broadcasting and writing about them. If I didn't know them personally, I knew that they were there, and I thought I knew where to find them. I *assumed* them. I knew that a city, even an empty one, is full of people who want to make things happen.

Having worked in big cities and regional centres, I'd never been involved with a call for proposals that wasn't oversubscribed. On simple extrapolation, I knew there were dozens, if not hundreds of people in Newcastle with an idea they were keen to act on. I'd not seen *anywhere* that wasn't full of people who were enthusiastic, self-starting and keen to take their own initiative. Everywhere I looked there was a surplus of talented motivated people looking for opportunities, and a deficit of opportunities, spaces, places to do them in.

What has always impressed me about creative people is less their role as trendsetters or tastemakers than their resourcefulness and resilience, their entrepreneurialism and their open-ended willingness to back an idea.

It is not that artists know better than anyone else, or are cooler. They aren't dramatically ahead of the curve and they certainly can't just sprinkle the magical fairy dust of 'creativity' over otherwise uninspired places. Such ideas are overrated in my opinion. What they *are,* in the broad sense, is willing to try new things. They are full of people who interested in trying things in situations where others might not.

Too often the way artists and creative communities are brought into city-building paradigms ignores this crucial element. They are engaged via consultation, or hired for aesthetics to build static artworks, monuments, icons and objects. It's not a bad thing, but it kind of misses the point.

While an aesthetically more interesting finished product in good public art is a good thing, and cultural facilities are an important part of any community's infrastructure, this strategy ignores a more immediate value: an artist's propensity to try things where others may not.

Operating on tiny budgets I learned you can do a lot with a little. I learned that there's a simple trade-off between control and autonomy. I've never had the resources to tell someone what kind of work to do, or to demand that they do *my* ideas for *me*. I discovered the trick of enabling the ideas of others, rather than trying to get others to implement mine.

People will take all manner of creative, personal and professional risks if you are willing to help them achieve *their* vision. You will pay a high premium for making their ambitions subservient to yours. But through choosing who and how to help you can gently curate and create a coherent set of possibilities.

Cities and festivals operate on different timescales. Festivals are immediate and intense. Cities evolve slowly. Even the most successful of cities spend long times in limbo because the timescales of their processes and planning produce long gaps. Buildings and sites can sit empty waiting for decisions for months, years or even decades. From the logic of the owners and developers, the uncertainty is a reason to do nothing.

But 'soon' has a completely different calibration on construction time than it does on festival production time. I have run an entire program in the time between committee meetings and report revisions.

The time required to extract value was different as well. Almost everything I had worked on ran for periods of a few days or weeks. The assumption that there was no value in the short-term made no sense to me. I'd worked on many projects that had paid themselves back, in cash or in kind or in opportunity and experience, in a single night or a short season.

They'd added much to the places and people who had been involved with them—and disappeared. Permanence isn't a prerequisite for generating value. For many it would be a burden. No one wants to keep their show open if no one is coming—each show is a rehearsal and launching point for the next one.

Temporariness opens up all prospects and possibilities, but you need to understand what it means to be temporary. What the particular costs and complexities are. What kind of investment of time or money or energy or expertise can be recouped in five or thirty or sixty days. What terms you need to offer for that to make sense and what expectations you can ask of someone needs to be proportionate to the reality of the resources.

In the festival world nothing requires much in the way of permanent infrastructure—you build and unbuild it as needed. You bring it with you and take it when you leave. Adaptability is crucial. You have to be able to build things that can be set up and dismantled, done and undone, packed and unpacked easily and cheaply.

In retail, an empty street or shopping centre is a disaster. In a festival it is simply an empty venue—everything starts that way. The audience is something you can bring with the event and grow by your actions. You don't look at a site for a music festival and judge its suitability by how many people are already there. You bring the people to the place with the activity.

Unlike retail, where there is a premium on visibility and passing trade, in this world if what you are doing is sufficiently compelling, if you promote it well enough and your audience is well enough defined, people will find it.

For most of the makers and artists I know it's not about money. It's not about certainty. It's about an opportunity for experimentation. Eventual success requires *first* that the price of failure is low enough that you can afford to follow dead ends. Projects need the flexibility to be iterative—to try ideas that might not work. They actually *need* to learn to fail cheaply and often and quickly enough to apply the experience and try again. You often realise why bad ideas are bad by doing them, and trying not to repeat your mistakes.

I have mostly worked outside the traditional arts infrastructure. I first organised exhibitions in scrounged spaces in Newcastle when I was 21. We set up temporary galleries in empty inner-city shops as part of a fringe festival that I started. Hundreds of people came out for the opening, but I mismanaged the supervision so badly that I look back mostly through a long mental list of mistakes not to repeat.

In Melbourne, with others, I started Australia's largest computer game developer's conference in a disused inner-city karate dojo. I've negotiated permits for performances in laneways, basements and on rooftops. I've organised street closures and juggled the noise implications of outdoor music stages. For one festival, we once filled a warehouse with forty-two stacked shipping containers, each enclosing a different artist-run gallery or project from around the world. We managed to do it while ensuring full wheelchair accessibility and juggling a complex engineering load. In short, I have spent a lot of time and gained a lot of practical experience negotiating the use of the city for others.

An architect or urban planner will see a city's challenges in terms of the things that need to be planned and new infrastructure that needs to be built. Engineers and administrators will look at the city from above. They see footpaths that need resurfacing, roads that need widening, traffic that needs speeding up or calming down, ways to encourage or discourage more cars and/or cycling and/or pedestrian circulation.

A museum or gallery director will see gleaming galleries and museums as catalysts for transformation of precincts, cities and towns. Cultural planners and place-makers may see a lack of public art, compelling details, community programs, and live events.

There's nothing wrong with any of these approaches. Each has its place. Executed well, they are each important, but they don't always address the problem. You can only solve so many problems by building and belting shinier newer louder nails. Some problems need hacksaws or, in my experience, duct tape and sweat. The problem is not that these roles and perspectives aren't important. It is that a lot of important things are no one's role.

That's not my hammer. For me the city has always been the fixed thing we work around. It is a constraint that is beyond our power to physically change more than peripherally. The question becomes not how to change the city, but how to creatively respond to it. I've never had the luxury of asking what a city should *ideally* be, but only to look at what it is and ask, *Who wants to do something here and what do they need to do it?*

I have always come at cities from the perspective of the user. Looking back, my trial-and-error training had shown me something that most never see. I'd worked with many users on different projects, across many jurisdictions, and across a variety of contexts and scales. I'd worked with people who were motivated but under-resourced. I'd seen what confronted them. I'd seen how they resolved, fudged, morphed or sidestepped their way through complex problems. I'd seen them fail and falter and I'd seen *why*.

In hindsight that skillset is rare. Most people will have only ever intersected with the doing processes—the dark matter of planning, the process of generating activity in any given space or place—only once or twice in their lifetime. A few people will have become specialists at doing the same things over and over again, whether it's building apartments or opening restaurants.

The only others who have repeatedly engaged in such spaces are well-paid consultants for companies, developers and entities with budgets for whom the solution to most problems is spending money. That wasn't an option here.

In retrospect, I had become an expert in adaptation, resourcefulness and experimentation. What I knew about was trying to do things. I knew people for whom infrastructure was something they had to make up as they went along, or adapt from what was readily available. I'd seen what makes doing things easy and what makes it hard.

I'd learned a lot about what it took for people to succeed, when they might give up or how they might adapt their needs and plans pragmatically when barriers appeared in their way. Most importantly of all, I began from a different assumption: that lots of people wanted to try stuff, and wouldn't need much to help them do it.

Part Two—

CHANGING FORTUNES

Chapter Five—

CHANGING CITIES

The 1970s, when I was born, is the last era that older Novocastrians nostalgise. The last high point before the decline set in; the last flicker before the city faded.

It is natural, I guess, to assume that the place and time that you grew up in is somehow an ideal, the *status quo* from which everything else has deviated, and that the city you were born into is as it always was or always should have been. But cities are dynamic places. They change. They change not just in simple lines and extrapolations, but in waves and in cycles.

Newcastle has been many places. It has had many dynamics and many economies. It has ridden the upside of a few great booms, and the downside of many longer busts. You can see it in the architecture and the buildings. You can see it vividly in old black-and-white Box Brownie prints and sepia-toned photos.

In old images it is easy to notice the superficial things. The unpaved roads and grand verandahs; familiar buildings in unfamiliar contexts. Ornate facades lost to history. The elaborate fashion, and the strange prevalence of late 19th Century proto-hipster beards.

Peer beyond the surface, and a layer that has long disappeared comes into view. In the late 1800s and early 1900s, a few short blocks on Hunter Street were home to a 'Boot & shoe manufactory,' a maker of 'Suits and tailoring, vests and trousers and hats,' a 'watchmaker and jeweller' proudly boasting "All work guaranteed," a 'confectioner,' a 'leather and grindery store,' and a 'wholesale and retail butcher' that by today's standards would be seen as a small abattoir.

One end of the street hosted a bicycle factory, which made car parts on request. You could stop in at an astonishingly large number of hotels and pubs selling concoctions brewed on the premises or in the neighbourhood nearby.

This is not the high street that I remember. It is a different place. A place for gathering and assembling, and the centre of social life. There are few national chains. It is almost all local business, with occasionally advertised brand names from afar. Newcastle at this time was not unique. At the beginning of the 20th century every city or town played host to many local and regional names and few, if any, global brands. Before the supermarket and the mega mall, the streets were for the bespoke and the boutique.

It wasn't really a place of retail, in the sense that I've always understood it, at all. Most of what was sold on those streets was actually made, repaired and prepared there. Shoes, tailored clothing, confectionary, leatherwork, watches and jewellery were all, as the norm, made or at least repaired and crafted within local communities.

The idea of an 'importer' was novel enough that large signs in big letters pointed this particular and peculiar service out. Making and manufacturing drove the logic and purpose of how these places evolved much more so than selling did.

This was true of Newcastle, but as you flick through old archival photos, the same could be said of pretty much any old main street, in any city, in almost any part of the world from that era. Before the rise of suburbs—before Ford, Taylorism, and mass manufacturing—main streets were places for creation as much as for consumption. The idea that goods are simply imported pre-packaged, marked up and sold with no value added at the local stage would have seemed unlikely and unusual.

Today such places are simply on the receiving end of a global chain of distribution. That local ecology of creation, social and civic life, interaction and connection has made way for places built largely for consumption.

It's not entirely gone. In some Asian cities you can still see the visible presence of makers, and small-scale industries remain a necessary part of the street life. In the West there are hold-out places where the visible presence of local makers and value-adders are still part of the story. You can still find butchers, bakers and restaurants—although many are simply distribution points for major chains—mixed in with the odd shoe repair shop, confectionary maker, tailor, jeweller.

In developing countries it is a necessity. In the West often it's a novelty, a luxury, or an archaic service. Often there is a premium on it, or at least on the veneer of having some sense of authenticity around.

For the most part though, such places have become rare

exceptions. Today's shopping centres and main streets are the local outposts of a global monoculture. They are indistinct and generic. Where they once had deep local roots, they now have global supply chains, franchises, branding and marketing. Local retailers have been out-scaled, swallowed up, bought out, merged into and marginalised by national and international chains. Many main streets—even as I understood them as a child—are gone or struggle to exist at all.

The centrifugal forces of suburban sprawl and car-centric planning, the logistics of distribution, and the price of land have driven retail and economic activity away to enclosed shopping centres and strip malls. Gone are the makers, the local retailers, and the gathering places. Our city, town, and old suburban centres are too often little more than an incoherent collection of chain stores, interchangeable discount shops, and empty facades.

Driving it all was something that has little to do with Newcastle, with shops or with retail. By the beginning of the 21st Century, global economies of scale had transformed manufacturing from something that took place locally to something that can just as likely take place on the other side of the country or the world. The places where we buy became interchangeable, while the places that make had become far off and invisible.

It is the paradox of 21st Century retail: every place offers greater choices than ever before, and yet increasingly, everywhere is like everywhere else. There is little variation to be found in the architecture of the flagship stores, or the brands and products that mid-range retailers sell, or even the cheap plastic junk in the dollar shops dotting suburban strips. You can find the same palate and products replicated hundreds, thousands, if not millions of times in places around the world.

Sepia-toned images remind us that it was not always like this. They capture a world far richer and more nuanced than the retail centres of today. Local storekeepers had larger-than-life personalities, family businesses passed down through generations, and almost everyone knew the radio jingle for local brands. It was swept up so quickly we have almost forgotten it was there, but a lot of it has happened in my lifetime.

Looking back it seems inevitable. But looking forward from half a century ago it is jarring to think how unlikely this must have seemed. These days, low labour costs and cheap transportation mean that everything from iPhones and high-end electronics to cheap plastic toys can be made in Communist China, and whisked almost frictionlessly to slick stores or bargain bins in Budapest, Sandton, or Adelaide. In virtually any city or its suburbs, you can drive straight into an air-conditioned shopping centre, load up, and get back into your car, and barely have to face an uncontrolled climate.

This global retail monoculture is the result of developments in economics, technology, politics, and finance. It was born from a moment in time seeded by shifts in transport, regulation, and global geopolitics, and begotten by the birth of suburbia, the rise of cheap credit, Deng Xiaoping's proclamation that "to get rich is glorious," international trade agreements, cost efficiencies in construction, containerization, and a communications revolution that has disrupted and accelerated virtually everything.

Chapter Six—

SHIPPING. SHOPPING. SHUTTING.

Under a single massive roof, the clean and pristine modern shopping experience offers up a cornucopia of consumption that brings together products and produce from everywhere on earth. But this experience is predicated on a kind of stability that physical places simply cannot offer. Cities are dynamic—they change.

Modern retail is a precarious, complex and interdependent system. It has many critical and interconnected parts. The rise of online shopping and the spluttering recovery from global recession have seen pieces begin to unravel.

America's malls (according to the *Wall Street Journal*) and Britain's 'once thriving shopping centres' (according to *The Daily Mail*) have become or are rapidly becoming ghost towns. In the UK, the five years from 2007 onwards saw 208 companies close or go into receivership. Between them, they had operated over 21,000 stores and employed over 187,000 people.

Australia was not exempt. In 2013, the business pages of *The Age* in Melbourne asked in response to rising vacancy rates and underwhelming sales figures—simply, and provocatively—'What's killing off retailing?'

The Internet has had a profoundly disruptive effect on the old retail business models. Just as the old Main Street declined with the rise of the car and the suburban shopping centre, there is another transformation underway. It has happened before and will happen again. The economics of how we make and shape places is being disrupted by another revolution in technology. Where until recently stuffing a median selection of everything into hundred stores or one massive one was the pinnacle of choice, today it is no longer enough.

We have lost Blockbuster, Borders and countless suburban book, music and video stores. They were vulnerable because the products themselves could be digitised and digitally delivered. Increasingly, every retail category in which the product is predictable, bulky, niche and un-perishable enough that it could purchased cheaper, held longer, presented better, or be more conveniently delivered or selected online has begun to follow.

Massive choice is giving way to infinite choice, and the logic of the logistics of our places has started to change. No shopping centre can ever offer the variety of Amazon. No retailers can match its economies of scale. They are wedged between the ubiquitous availability of staples and the sheer variety and diversity of a global marketplace where every maker, every factory, every artisan, every hobbyist, and every craftsperson is present in every home.

Retail—or at least a lot of the infrastructure we've built for it—is interdependent. Every shop relies on the ones around it to attract customers, to bring foot traffic, and to inspire serendipitous discovery.

Today's retail strips and shopping centres increasingly resemble a game of Jenga or KerPlunk—where each empty shop, every boarded up or hoarded facade, every missing retail chain removed from the structure makes it harder and harder on the businesses around it. Every missing piece makes it increasingly likely that the edifice will come crashing down.

A system that once refined and nearly perfected the process of shipping predictable, marketable products from anywhere to you, via convenient intermediate points, is becoming obsolete. All those points at which an intermediary clipped the ticket as products were housed, inspected, displayed and sold have become luxuries that can no longer be afforded.

All the jobs they generated are going with them. It is a case study in creative destruction just as vivid as the decline of the local 'mom and pop' store was a generation or two earlier, and the end of the local maker-manufacturer was a generation or two before that.

But what does it mean for our cities, our streets and our places? Through the prism of now, it is difficult to see how much of our urban and suburban ecology, of the design and dynamics of our cities is built on the logic of this particular kind of global production chain.

Hidden in plain sight is the other great paradox of 21st Century retail. As our streets, our towns, our cities and communities have become more and more alike, our inner lives have become more and more different. We have more choice—near infinite choice—in how we create ourselves.

This choice extends to the things we buy, the music we listen to, the clothes we wear, the media we consume, the news we pay attention to, the ideological bubbles we live in and the facts we choose to believe, the sports we obsess over, the games we play and the diets we follow.

It's as though all the world's cultures exist everywhere simultaneously and we can increasingly pick and choose the pieces that we wish to exist within us. We can make, shape and curate ourselves, our identities, and our influences from an infinite constellation of reference points.

For our cities and our communities, it's a trap. There is a growing tension between the diversity enabled by our electronic interconnectedness and the predictability of our physical environments.

It is possible to wake up in a hotel room, as I have done in Asia, South America, the US and Europe and Australia, look out the window and see a McDonald's, a KFC or a Starbucks, and then struggle to identify which continent, let alone which city, you are in. In many cities and many suburbs it has become increasingly difficult to tell simply by looking where—if anywhere—you actually are.

Our physical communities are increasingly competing with our virtual ones for time, attention, and the investment of our efforts, our interests and our energies. The expectations of diversity and possibility seeded by the virtual world are shut out of the physical one. As cities, civic leaders and place-makers grapple with the global forces of technology, changing dynamics and economics of places, they must also grapple with micro ones: with the local eruption of new ideas and expectations.

Chapter Seven—

AN ERUPTION OF POSSIBILITY

With the choice of offerings diminished, and local and global retailers virtually indistinguishable in their merchandise, it was perhaps inevitable that customers would take things into their own hands.

In Australia, in the first half of the first decade of the 21st Century, something statistically improbable began to happen, across towns and suburbs, bedrooms and sheds, in both the city and the countryside. In fact it was happening around the world, but the statisticians at the Australian Bureau of Statistics were in the right place, at the right time and asking the right questions to make sense of it. With little fanfare—then or since—they caught one of the great creative awakenings of any time in human history.

In just six years, between 2001 and 2007, the number of Australians working full-time or part-time across a range of creative fields exploded. Design grew by 31%; crafts 163%;

drawing 348%; and jewellery an astonishing 672%. The full spectrum of creative fields that the Bureau was monitoring erupted, with double- or triple-digit rates of growth in barely a handful of years.

I can imagine the statisticians checking and second-guessing their numbers, turning pages upside down, recalibrating graphs and questioning data points, and searching in vain for the misplaced decimal points. But what they had captured was real, a seismic shift in creative practice. They had captured a once-in-a-generation, perhaps once-in-a-century transition.

The fall of big retailers had coincided with—or triggered—the rise of a new boutique economy. A global market now existed for what had once been the isolated and isolating practices of local creativity. Within a small number of years, dozens of previously tiny isolated forms of creativity and culture practiced by hundreds of thousands of Australians were transformed by global economies of scale.

Such cultures have always been there. In my student years, Newcastle was a great do-it-yourself town—largely by necessity. It wasn't a world of flashy gallery openings or slick major venues. It was a culture of improvisation and necessity; of local bands in decaying pubs; visual artists of varying quality; part-time poets and playwrights; jury-rigged fashion and vegan video-makers; cask wine and improvised design. It was cheap, undercapitalised, and overenthusiastic.

With few exceptions, it was a mostly-local community, and mostly without much of a market. For most, it was hobby or an ambition. Art or music was rarely a job, even a part-time one, significant enough to bother the statisticians. It was a gift and barter economy where most transactions were settled in favours, food, or cases of beer.

Such cultures are not always obvious but if you knew where to look you could likely have found similar scenes in most places. There have always been pockets of creativity across virtually any country town, city, or suburb. Contrary to certain assumptions, this isn't particularly an urban, 'hipster' or youthful phenomenon. You can find similar dynamics, dabblers, and part-time creativity across many demographics.

There have always been people working on their music, photographers, carpenters and wood-turners, knitters and sewers, jewellers, designers, artists and artisans, makers and creators of varying levels of commitment and quality in every community. Suddenly they had access to an audience.

The problem, historically, was that there was never much of a market. It wasn't always one of quality or talent, but of complexity of distribution. A hand-crafted pendant, no matter how distinctive the aesthetic and how well-made, would struggle to sell more than a few copies in all but the largest of local communities.

For most, the cost of seeking out a market further afield for such a low-volume object was prohibitively expensive. Even if the design and production were exquisite, the marketing, shipping, and transaction costs of finding an audience spread across the country and around the world were frighteningly prohibitive.

Then, virtually overnight, that problem disappeared. The internet is to the craft and design market as the iPhone is to the smoke signal. At any given time, it is a 24/7 global marketplace of handmade objects, a global distributor of unsigned bands, a permanent shop window of undiscovered photography.

Grandma's lovingly crafted doilies are still there, but they sit in online stores next to hand-embroidered laptop bags, cult creatures, offensive objects and intricate jewellery made from recycled junk.

In an instant of statistical time, makers the world over began connecting with their peers, with inspiration, with tools and tutorials and, most importantly, with markets and audiences. Importantly, this kind of creativity has often been motivated less by economic returns than by the economically irrational motivations of creativity and possibility. Never had the price of participation been lower. With the drop in costs and explosive growth in markets the landscape had changed almost instantly.

In Etsy's headquarters in Brooklyn, there's a mesmerising real time map of transactions on a rotating globe of the world. A constant series of arcs connect sellers and buyers between Newcastle and New Zealand, Sydney and Shanghai, Melbourne and Montana. By late 2013, Etsy was the world's largest handmade marketplace, selling nearly US$150 million dollars a month worth of handmade objects to tens of millions of members. Each month it was generating more than 2 billion page views.

Where once Australia had suffered from the 'tyranny of distance,' where even our most successful artists struggled to make a name for themselves internationally without physically making the move to Los Angeles, London, or New York, now 70% of Etsy's Australian sales were international exports. We are local makers with a global market.

It is not only those distributing online that benefit from the rapidly falling costs of distribution and communication. Want to find a store to stock your product on the opposite side of the world? The capacity to reach out to and collaborate has never been cheaper. Want to wrangle a presence at a national or international fashion festival, a market, or a trade fair? Promotional opportunities have come a long way from the days when you had to pre-book and pay for an expensive trunk telephone call.

As traditional retail centres have faltered and crumbled, in part thanks to the disruptive power of the internet, a new invisible economy has emerged. With the help of third-party aggregators and intermediaries taking a small percentage of profits, small-scale makers and creators have developed a direct maker-to-buyer online business model.

It is at once a shift back to the business values of a hundred years ago—where you knew the name of the person who made your clothes—and a leap forward to a global neighbourhood, where the fact that person is on opposite side of the world is almost irrelevant.

Too often the business press talks about technology as though it is about buzzwords, gadgets, IPOs, large-scale disruptive transformations and billions of dollars worth of value created or destroyed. For most of us, it is the banal, almost invisible transformations, the clustering of small possibilities rather than the marketing of big ones, that have made lasting changes.

It is the things we do every day that we forget were recently impossible. Often the tiny aggregated activities of the smallest of us are most substantial.

The economic change has brought with it a cultural one. Being creative in a small town or a regional city is no longer an isolating or eccentric activity. Networks, communities, appreciative fans and markets reach well beyond the physical boundaries of any place.

In small towns across regional Australia, the story of that girl whose bags were bought by someone in Prague, or the guy whose wallets were featured in an international blog or magazine, confers legitimacy where there would once have been disinterest. Such people can now bring money into the local economy from outside, and not merely compete for or recycle the meagre resources that are already there.

As these communities have emerged, grown and matured, a whole ecosystem has grown up around them. Design markets and craft fairs. Networks of ideas, raw materials, promotion, curation and inspiration. It is no longer complex to order specialist supplies, or to learn how a particular process or technique is done. It is easier than ever to find a teacher or a tutor, or someone to custom-manufacture the elements that you, yourself, cannot.

As the marketplace has become more globalised it has also become more diverse, more subcultural and much less hierarchical. Fashion and design once filtered down and out from creative producers living in Los Angeles, Tokyo, Shanghai, London or New York. To some extent it still does, but that dynamic now coexists with a constellation of creators, critics, and producers spread widely around the world.

Niches from farm workwear to gothic millinery have emerged, and new technology links buyers to sellers, and makers to collectors, curators and connoisseurs, despite the burdens of geography. Once being from regional Australia may have been a problem. Today regional variation and local identity are all part of the story. Being from *somewhere* can become a powerful resource. Distinctiveness or even a peculiar local kitsch that might once had been a liability is now an asset if handled well.

Despite rates of growth that would make Chinese railway engineers ashamed, this transformation has taken place almost entirely under the radar of traditional retailers and policy-makers. At a time when the economic and cultural dynamics of invisible communities are becoming more diversified than ever, many of our visible communities were heading in the exact opposite direction.

Very little of this change was trickling up. This creative impulse has the potential to be a driver of experimentation and distinctiveness, with ever-lowering barriers to entry online spurring a surge of participation and innovation. Meanwhile, in most places, the barriers to entry in our physical environment were growing higher and more complex than ever.

What was missing in many communities were the entry points. Our towns and cities were wasting their most precious resource: the initiative and imagination of their citizens.

Chapter Eight—

THE BIG FIX

I'm not sure what it is about struggling cities that makes them so tempted by grand solutions, mega-projects and Hail Mary passes. Perhaps it is simply the scale of the shocks, but debates about revitalisation often become preoccupied with large-scale change. Perhaps its inevitable that with the loss of a single large-scale industry like a steelworks, the default assumption is that renewal would best be served by replacing it with something at least symbolically of similar scale.

But there is nothing more precarious for the long-term economic vitality than being a single-industry town. War and natural catastrophes aside, most stories of dying cities are cautionary tales about the dangers of relying on a single company or depending on a single industry. Whether it's Newcastle and the BHP Steelworks, Detroit and the car industry, or the old Soviet Bloc centres of research or manufacturing, the pattern is often the same.

In regional towns stories are often similar but on a smaller scale. A single meat packing plant, a cannery, a sale yard, a mine, a particular tourism market that had once driven the growth of place can easily become catalysts of their collapse.

Large projects are a terrible risk-mitigation strategy, and yet they are the first place that most leaders go looking to for reassurance. I have lost track of how many such schemes have come and gone in Newcastle over the last few decades.

These have included casinos, a new steelworks, a mega-tower that would rise thirty stories above the empty streets and—my personal favourite—building Sydney's second airport on industrial land at Kooragang Island, land so unnecessarily close to the city that the residents and businesses of Newcastle would have endured the constant sound of jet noise. In the late '80s or early '90s there was actually, really, honestly a serious proposal to save the city centre by building... a monorail.

Politically, the idea of a single development is a tempting and convenient prop. It is easy to rally for or against. It's sound-bite answer to what is inevitably a complicated mercurial question. It guarantees a media story and satisfies the perceived need to be doing something. Anything.

This is not a feature unique to one or other side of politics. The left still tends towards large state-centric and government investments. The right is seduced by the magic of private investment and global capital, so much so it is often willing to underwrite risks, cut taxpayer-funded deals or forgo revenues as might be necessary to attract or leverage it. Politics in general is rarely adept at thinking small, promising little, and acting iteratively.

Incremental but navigable challenges are reduced to big binary decisions, a constant series of crises and tipping points. Cities in desperate need of revitalisation are often littered with the carcasses of grand ambitions now deflated, or yearning holes where the fruit of architect's impressions were supposed to have been.

This is not to say big ideas are inherently bad. There are many good big ideas. There are many practical and viable projects. The major problem with most of them is not that they are bad, but that they are they are often a distraction. At best, they aren't going to happen quickly. If my experience is anything to go by, most of them aren't going to happen at all.

In Newcastle, most such proposals are highly polarising. They are often in need of capital the local community doesn't actually have. Big projects bring with them big risks, big budgets, and big temptations. In 2014, after decades of fits and starts, of failed developments, backflips and reneged deals, Newcastle's entire urban renewal strategy hiccoughed yet again as a corruption scandal cost the city its Mayor, two members of the state parliament, and a yet-to-be-measured amount of momentum.

In Newcastle today there are plans underway to relocate much of the suburban university campus into the old city centre. The state government may or may not be in the process of removing the much-debated heavy rail line into the city—either a vital public transport link or an impenetrable barrier that splits the city in half, depending on which side you line up on—and replacing it with light rail. A fast train to Sydney has been mooted yet again to eventually replace the rambling and decrepit pre-20th Century era service colloquially known as the Shitkansen.

The development of a large-scale 'cultural precinct' with an expanded gallery and museum has been on-again off-again on-again, and the next stage is currently off. A major retail and residential development in and around the city's mall is, at time of writing, somewhere between a green light, on hold, and in limbo. Many of these plans have been around in some form or another for at least fifteen years.

Watching such plans come and go can you make you jaded. Over several decades many such schemes have come and gone. Some have failed. Many have merit. Some have succeeded to a modest extent. Some have done more harm than good. Most have disappeared or been delayed indefinitely.

Some of the more spurious ones were little more than the fantasies of monorail-spruiking hucksters taking a city in dire need of hope for a ride. In twenty years and counting, none have proved the single simple catalyst for a reversal of fortunes that their proponents claim and citizens crave.

It is not a comment on the merits of any of these ideas individually to observe that, collectively, they create an illusion that keeps deferring the future. They push change over the horizon to some future time when the big things are fixed and the little things will follow. Newcastle's big city centre revitalisation is three-to-five years away. It always has been.

Part of the problem is the seduction of infrastructure—the desire to buy and build things. The idea is that new edifices are needed to bring new industries that will fill them. It is not uncommon to see big public investments in building more and newer things while old ones simply sit despairingly unused. Or to see government buying up iconic vacant properties because they have to be seen, politically, to be doing something, and then sending them into the purgatory of committees and consultants and plans and processes while everyone waits for something to actually happen.

Perhaps I am simply impatient—restless. But I am not one to look over the horizon at the expense of what is happening at my feet. Amid the daily debates about developments and daydreams, amid the front-page stories and artist illustrations, between the conceptual drawings and the master plans, in Newcastle in 2008 no one really seemed to notice that real estate agents weren't returning phone calls.

It wasn't really anyone's job to notice. City revitalisation agendas were full of master-planners looking at hard infrastructure, transport plans, height limits, large-scale zoning and development controls. They spoke with investors, bankers, entrepreneurs and industrialists. With people who thought and talked big.

While it sounds ambitious, too often it is a cover, the result of thinking small and looking backwards, to another steelworks; to the big names and brand retailers than have fled to the suburbs, and to the comfort and certainties of another time and ambitions of another era. It is easy to become so concerned with attracting capital at the grand scale that we never bother to ask how the city functions for those without it.

Meanwhile there was a quiet crisis of the small stuff. 2008 was defined by a growing dynamic of small ambitions and networked opportunities. If a place is to thrive and succeed in an era of atomised and independent activity, it needs to look down, not just up. It helps to step back from the big ideas, come down from the boardroom, down to street level and look around and observe how well it is working there. If it isn't working, you need to ask, *why not*?

The problem is not that there isn't value in attracting major investors and large-scale businesses and industries—each of those proposals can be judged on their merits. But they are the wrong point from which to *start*. Looking two, five or ten years ahead can blind you to the needs and possibilities of today, tomorrow, and the next day.

Good zoning, transport, infrastructure, street furniture, infrastructure and all those other 'hardware problems' are a vital part of the good planning of a healthy city. But so too is the less tangible but far more immediate need for people with ideas *to be able to do things*.

It is obvious, though often impertinent and uncomfortable to point out, that cities in transition need experiments and discovery much more than they need certainty and scale. Most planners and civic leaders don't actually know what will work. It is far more important not to ask not what the big answer is, but instead to unearth the little questions.

By the middle of 2008 several thoughts had begun to crystallise. I was beginning to question the whole narrative of Newcastle, why it was the way it was. As a result, I had begun to come to very different conclusions about what could be done about it. Resilient communities are ones where a diversity of scales, of interests and economic activity coexist. They are not ones looking only to the next big industry, company or scheme to make or break the place.

The problem had, at least to some extent, been misdiagnosed. At the level I was looking, what was seen as a lack of interest and demand was a far more complicated web of poor processes, bad incentives and bad systems. There was a structural misunderstanding that blinded the city's planners to the possibilities and opportunities of the present.

It was simply not the case that buildings sat empty because no one wanted to use them, or even because there weren't potential viable uses for them. There was a mismatch between the resources and expectations required to utilise them and the assumptions of those who controlled the process, both government and private.

It was as though there were a series of gears, cogs and wheels that weren't quite the right shape for each other—all turning, grinding, and some furiously spinning. Collectively at best they were only lurching forward in erratic bursts. Often they were going nowhere.

The big idea that was forming was that maybe the biggest priority wasn't a big idea after all—that we needed to think about the problems at a smaller and not a greater scale. Not, *How do you motivate and incentivise the big thing that will fix everything?* but instead, *How do you reduce the problems down to size so that individuals and small groups of people can tackle them with their own efforts?*

Newcastle's problem was apparently so large that it could only be fixed by a catalytic transformation, a big investment brought in and resourced from outside. Peering in the windows of dozens and dozens of empty shops and trying to rent them, the problem seemed so small that it couldn't.

It was actually hundreds of little problems, each one of them capable of being transformed by the application of imagination, enthusiasm, and sweat equity. Rightly or wrongly, I confidently believed there were people who wanted to do that.

Part Three—

UNLIKELY OPPORTUNITIES

Chapter Nine—

BEERS AND IDEAS

I was once on a conference panel with a group of 'place leaders' talking about the role and mechanics of culture in place-making, precincts and urban revitalisation. Someone in the audience asked us all how the organisations that we worked for had been founded and funded.

One had been formed as a result of a high-level government enquiry. Two had been formed by acts of state parliaments. One was created by spinning off tens of millions of dollars worth of government property assets into a new legal authority. Renew Newcastle, I explained, began over a few too many beers, was seed funded on my credit card, and was founded in the office of a guy called Rod.

It was a line too good to resist. In reality most ideas—at least for me—don't just arrive in a single origin moment. There is rarely a lightening bolt. They sort of percolate into being without ever consciously being intended.

I had been thinking about empty buildings in Newcastle for fifteen years. I'd first seen the opportunity in them way back in 1996, when I'd first borrowed that first bunch of empty shops for artists on a handshake deal. I'd been conscious of the problems and the practicalities since I'd cleaned up the consequences of that loose arrangement and some of their excesses in the aftermath.

Like many of my recurring obsessions it had been discovered, forgotten, and rediscovered many times. By the mid 2000s my concerns and interests had moved on to other things, but Newcastle kept reappearing in them. I had another life in Melbourne. I was getting married and planning on starting a family. I was directing larger festivals with bigger budgets, and making something of a name for myself in a wider world.

When I got the opportunity to write and present a national TV series on ABC television I worked in a bit of Newcastle. *Not Quite Art* was an essay-style provocation around ideas of what culture is and where it comes from. Shooting in early 2007, the first episode riffed off the idea of bottom-up versus top down-culture.

It compared iconic culture centres like Melbourne's Federation Square and the Sydney Opera House with the more pragmatic problems of places like Newcastle and Glasgow. In a later episode, I managed to work in an extended piece about the cultural impact of the state's ridiculous liquor licensing laws.

Outside of Newcastle, I had stumbled into prominence in and preoccupation with another argument, one that the show was about. Not that it got me anywhere, but I'd become increasingly outspoken about arts policy and funding. I'd argued that archaic, ageing, and institutional arts policy models were missing the point, that they failed to meet actual artists and their needs.

I was irritated that they pooled in a handful of large companies and institutions, and that they had gradually moved over decades from supporting artists who actually *made* things to subsidising middle managers of increasingly irrelevant infrastructures.

Those ideas were a recurring theme of the newspaper column I was writing for *The Age* in Melbourne. They came to a head when I was commissioned by editor Julianne Schultz to write a piece for a city-themed edition of the influential literary and policy journal, *Griffith REVIEW.*

Reading back now, the essay 'Fluid Cities Create' reads like a manifesto for what became Renew Newcastle. It wasn't meant to be. It predates even the idea of Renew by more than a year, and was written at a time when I had no intention of actually *doing* anything.

At the time that it was written, that was the furthest thing on my mind. It was a job with an interesting brief: write a four- or five-thousand-word piece about culture and cities. As it turned out, I had strongly-held ideas and opinions from my years of watching Newcastle crumble that I hadn't realised that I had. I wrote them down for the first time because for the first time, someone had asked me to.

What happened next was somewhere between fortuitous, unexpected and increasingly insane. I had gone back to Newcastle with the hope of opening a bar, and instead left with a different seed planted. My writing, broadcasting, and thinking completely failed to influence decision makers and policy makers, but it drew people out of the woodwork. It gradually introduced me to friends, colleagues, and acquaintances who became my future collaborators.

Then, one fateful night at a small pub in Sydney, a mutual friend suggested that I have a drink with someone I knew of but had never met before. Craig Allchin had been a significant figure in Australia's last great urban resuscitation—or at least the one that had most inspired me. As a young partner in the architecture firm Six Degrees they'd established Meyers Place—the first and among the most iconic of Melbourne's early small laneway bars.

The firm had been instrumental in many ground-breaking projects that had been part of a cultural sea change in Melbourne. They had helped set a template, and revealed possibilities that dozens of other places had acted upon. Craig was then living in Sydney working as a consultant to the City of Sydney and the New South Wales planning department, working on the formal policy and advocacy side of many of the ideas I'd been exploring and expressing. I wanted to pick his brain.

When we met, Craig was carrying that edition of *Griffith REVIEW.* He'd recently returned from Newcastle. His wife, the author Anna Funder, had been there to speak at the National Young Writers Festival, the same festival that I had started a decade earlier and had been involved in running for five or six years.

For the first time in my life I had a chance to talk aloud, at length, about Newcastle with someone who saw the same dynamics and possibilities as I did, who understood instinctively and intellectually the ideas I was trying to convey, and who was in a position to actually help me do something about them.

Craig offered his advice, his reputation, and his time. He offered to help in any way he could. Most of all, he just made me feel like I knew what I was doing—that I might be onto something. By the time last drinks were called I had decided to take him up on his offer. My plan was instant and obvious. I would return to Newcastle over the next few months and devote my time to solving the empty shop problem by...making a TV show about it.

There's an irony that a project designed in part around making failure easy began itself from a failed idea. I'd written and presented two moderately successful short television series, and was being asked for ideas for a third one. The *Not Quite Art* episode that featured Newcastle had gone down well. There was a trend for reality-based make-over feel good-style TV programming, so why not make over a city?

I also figured, somewhat cynically, that the best chance I'd ever get of anyone giving me their empty buildings would be if had a camera crew in tow.

I pitched a concept. The ABC was interested enough to encourage me to develop it. I'd envisioned a made-for-television fly-on-the-wall reality series, the camera following my fraught and frustrated adventures to convince the Mayor, a bunch of property owners and others to lend us some empty buildings to do some kind of makeover and exhibition. We'd spruce up the town while giving an eclectic group of well-cast artists a once-in-a-lifetime opportunity to have their own galleries. Think drama, tension, and weekly cliff-hangers.

For the camera, I was envisioning a bunch of reality TV tropes. *Will they be able to get the shops at all? Will James get his personal shit together in time for the opening? Will they get the power on in time or get shut down by the safety guys?* It would all end after half-a-dozen episodes with a civic makeover, a spectacular reveal, and a none-too-subtle point about how it's a good thing to let people do this stuff.

My producer liked it. The network's Executive Producer seemed to like it. It spent months in network purgatory before someone further up the chain killed it. I suspect it died because of budget and because in large part it was too much of a long shot. The drama of reality TV is mostly manufactured. Will they or won't they get hold of some empty shops is great drama. But you want to actually know the answer before you commit to making a program about it.

Fortunately death comes slowly in television. By the time it had come, the research had actually required me to think about the real practical questions. *If we were going to take a bunch of buildings, how would we do that? What were the legal implications? How would we deal with the planning and permission processes? How long and on what terms could we realistically get the properties for?*

These were questions I had tripped across individually but never really thought about systematically. I started to think about the precedents, realise more and more about the constraints, and began to seek out the people who could help me solve the problems.

I spoke to a lot of people. Though I wasn't actually an expert on urban planning, cities, culture, legals, or even art for that matter, the fact that I was proposing to play one on television more than compensated for my shortcomings. By the time I realised I wasn't actually making a TV series I felt like I'd raised a lot of people's expectations.

There's a perception that everyone wants to be on television, but the people involved in Newcastle were far more interested in the idea than in the show. In the end, it seemed neither here nor there that the TV part might not actually be going to happen. The TV show was a means to an end, and other pathways to that end were starting to reveal themselves.

Apart from Craig, the other most significant relationship at that time came from another unexpected dead end. I was out of my depth when it came to the legal implications of what I wanted to do. In a stroke of good timing, the New South Wales Arts Law Centre, a not-for-profit that gives free legal advice to artists, brought me up from Melbourne to speak on a panel about media arts and copyright—it had been a theme of one of my TV programs and some of my writing—and I took the opportunity to ask a favour in return.

Surely they could find me a *pro bono* lawyer? I needed someone to help with the legal complexities of a temporary space utilisation model that I'd begun to sketch out, not just with the agreements and insurances, but with insanely boring practical questions like whether it should be a company or an incorporated association, the risks and liabilities, what we could and couldn't practically ask of and offer to property owners.

As an Arts Law question, it was a bit beyond what the NSW Arts Law Centre legal services are usually asked for. Giving copyright advice when someone uses your picture without permission on a t-shirt was one thing. Renegotiating and reinventing the complex idiosyncrasies of the property industry was in other category entirely. It was beyond the scope of their office, but they offered to see if they could find one of their partner firms to take it on.

A few weeks later they called me back. They rattled off a who's who list of large legal firms that occasionally offered *pro bono* support to artists. Then they explained, in the kind of excruciating detail that lawyers can effortlessly slip into, why each and every one of them wasn't available or interested.

I'd begun to despair. There are ways around most things but the law—at least in this case—wasn't one of them. And it wasn't something I could afford to pay for. Lawyers charge by the hour the kind of budgets I'm used to spending in a week.

Then, almost as an afterthought, the one last thing they suggested to try was ROD. I assumed they were a firm or a service, and that ROD was an acronym. My initial response was, "Who are *they*?"

But Rod was a person. A young lawyer, he was working for Sparke Helmore —not a major Arts Law Centre partner but Newcastle's largest home-grown legal firm. It was a firm with no particular arts bent, but one that had a reputation, on occasions, of supporting good causes in the local community. Rod had once volunteered in their Sydney office as an intern and they said that they would give him a call.

Roderick Smith, as it would turn out, was one of the best kindred spirits and collaborators whose paths I've ever had the good fortune to cross. It didn't start out that way. Our initial phone conversations were stilted and awkward. I was in Melbourne, still underemployed and often in my pyjamas. I was doing my best to sound like I was professional enough to not be wasting the time of a proper law firm.

Rod, for his part, was carefully building a case. He was trying to convince Sparke Helmore's senior partners to allow him and the firm to take this on as a *pro bono* project. Eventually they agreed. Meanwhile, somewhat awkwardly, Rod was dropping the occasional hint that he too was an artist, that he played in a band and exhibited artwork on the side. He promised to send me a CD. My initial reaction was to be slightly terrified. I tried to think up some generic nice things to say about the music my lawyer was making.

It was two months or more before Rod and I met in person. Sparke Helmore's office was on the top floor of a shiny new building on Newcastle's rapidly redeveloping waterfront. It looked out across panoramic views of the harbour and across to the miles of sand dunes, bushland and golden beaches that stretch up to Port Stephens. I sat, waiting, feeling awkwardly like a defendant or unfortunate litigant on the wrong end of their expertise.

I needn't have feared. The man who walked in looked less like the corporate lawyer I feared and more like the musician he told me he was. It was the last meeting of the day. We waded through an intimidating pile of documents. I got a half hour *pro bono* seminar on corporate governance structures, liabilities and property law.

I'm not sure who suggested it but afterwards Rod and I headed to the pub together. Stilted conversation gave way to a rollicking and increasingly drunken tour of some Newcastle pubs. We peered in dozens of empty shop windows. We discovered that we shared many cultural reference points, some mutual friends, and similar frustrations and ambitions for the city.

Even the music thing turned out okay. Rod's then band Firekites had written songs I was already familiar with. I'd heard them on the radio and knew some of the other band members. Artists I knew had made their film clips. Rod knew empty spaces too. His band's first album had taken its name, 'The Bowery,' from the empty Art Deco-era inner-city Newcastle building that they'd recorded it in.

By the time we reached the last of the 'For Lease' signs we hugged, bounced ideas off each other, and drunkenly declared that the 'someone' who really should do something about the problems of the empty city was going to be us.

Chapter Ten—

SYSTEM FAILURE

On sober reflection, it probably shouldn't be us. It is one thing to express an opinion about what everyone else should be doing after a few drinks, or to write an article or make a TV series about how the world is supposed to work. It's quite another to actually find yourself doing it.

Given my obvious and instinctive sense of the ability of small communities, groups and individuals to solve problems for themselves, it is ironic that I spent a good ten or fifteen years trying to convince governments to do it for them. Even as we were embarking on Renew, I still believed that we would have to do it through or with government. I wanted them to *at least* make it easier.

I have a decidedly mixed relationship to politics. At times I fantasise about being Mayor or a politician, but then realise that I mostly lack the basic patience to sit through a council meeting.

I have often had it back to front. Until comparatively

recently I genuinely believed that any material change in a place needed to start with its politics. That there were good guys and bad guys, who mostly (but not always) split neatly along party or ideological lines. Us and them. If enough of the good guys got in, they'd somehow solve our problems for us. Obviously, it's more complex than that.

I've always been very interested in policy though. Through festival work, through media and arts advocacy, and in thinking about empty spaces, I developed a long wish-list of laws to change, reforms to implement, and programs and funding pools that should have existed.

I wanted incentives; carrots for donors of empty properties, and sticks in the form of punitive powers to force those who neglected them to do something. I wanted planning processes to be streamlined, consents to be sped up, and complexities to be relaxed. I wanted funding. I always want funding. I still do.

I wanted investment in the small stuff. I wanted leadership. I wanted the city council to transform itself from impenetrable bureaucracy to one-stop-shop for people who couldn't figure things out for themselves. I wanted elected officials to lead a cultural change. I wanted bureaucrats on salaries—and *not* volunteers—to seed and lead the grunt work.

I may as well have wanted rainbows, puppies and pandas.

I was consulted with enough to have become cynical of consultation. Back when I'd lived in Newcastle, I'd lost count of how many times I'd been asked for my opinion on what the city should do—how many meetings, workshops and presentations I'd attended. I'd seen dozens of experts brought in from outside with plans and proposals that ranged from the inspiring, to the unrealistic, inept, irrelevant, tone-deaf and utterly ignorant.

I'd long argued that small-scale creative enterprise should be a key element in the city's future. After all, if a bunch of kids like us could build up a DIY arts and media festival into the city's largest tourism event, then what could be done with a serious plan and some actual resources?

Through the eyes of people who came to town for the This Is Not Art festival, Newcastle's empty spaces were an amazing opportunity. Newcastle's future had to get beyond the big development-type thinking. At one point the festival got a little bit of money to do a property guide for 'creatives', but for the most part I was putting forward an answer to a question that no one was actually asking.

Yet when I returned to Newcastle in 2008 to begin my TV project/Renew experiment, I was convinced it would be different. After all I had serious allies. I had a national profile. I had been on television! I had a lawyer. Surely someone would be listening this time.

What had improved was my ability to get meetings. I was able to meet with national, state and local governments. I met with elected officials and public servants. Some got it. Some glazed over. There was at least a little interest.

I attempted to convince whoever I was talking to and whoever would listen that the city or the state could take the lead on this. I found examples from around the world of what they could do.

In parts of the United Kingdom, they provide deductions on council taxes for charities to occupy otherwise vacant properties. In Melbourne's early 1990s recession the council had relaxed its planning laws to encourage cheap activity in the city. Other places had fast-tracked their compliance and permit processes (or even gotten council inspectors to proactively help start new things!) so that creative ideas with limited capital could happen quickly.

The council could use its long-term leverage with developers—after all, they would need to approve future developments—to encourage short-term activation. Most importantly, governments themselves were among the largest owners of vacant properties—surely council- or state-owned buildings could be the first to be temporarily activated? Failing any of that, how about just writing us a cheque and I'll try and somehow get on with it?

Initially this headway seemed quite promising. Just being able to get the meetings encouraged me to persevere. But over time it became apparent that behind the veneer of engagement, very little was actually happening. I realise now I have never been good at this side of things. I've never been great at applying strategic pressure, forcing policy changes or unlocking buckets of money.

Lobbying is tiring, time-consuming and resource-intensive. It steals valuable time away from actually doing things. Even five years later, it is really only the funding that has actually improved—even that comes in waves and seemingly lurches from crisis to crisis. All of those bigger policy suggestions and solutions are still in the too-hard basket.

For all the general interest in the idea at a conceptual level, there was always a reason to not actually do anything about it *now*. Because the department was in the midst of (yet another) restructure; because someone seemed to think that they'd already done it or had a report on it (they hadn't); because they insisted that they couldn't; because there was an election coming up or just past; or because such problems were part of yet *another* plan that needed to be finalised before any actual action could take place.

Structurally, there was an even bigger problem. The problems as I had come to understand them weren't the result of any *one* thing. The city's dysfunction seemed to resemble some kind of Rubik's Cube, where no one piece could move independently. It was an accumulation of the unintended consequences of decisions made across three levels of government over dozens and probably hundreds of years.

Whether well-intentioned or simply as an excuse, there was an awful lot of, "I can't move my bit because their bit is in the way," or "If I change this I will have to change all these other things as well," and a legitimate fear of invoking new unintended consequences.

To unpack these wicked problems at the level of politics and power would require the engagement of dozens of agencies, and the stakeholders that existed within those various governments. The siloing of roles and responsibilities both within and between these agencies and organisations meant that despite all the goodwill in the world, most of the problems identified were everyone's problem and no one's. To fix them would require coordination and leadership from the highest level—and I haven't met that leader yet.

At several key points there didn't seem to be any understanding or interest in offering any support. Some key players were in denial that there was even a problem at all, let alone that there was an opportunity.

Newcastle's then Mayor actively tried to discourage me. He warned me that I was "talking the city down." He denied the city even *had* a problem with empty buildings. He seemed to genuinely believe that if you didn't draw attention to the vacancies and blight in the city centre, maybe no one would notice them. He was concerned that it would only serve to deter investment and send the city's reputation backwards.

It was, to put it mildly, an interesting argument. Perhaps it might have had some validity if the problems were short-term and recent and no one had noticed. But they weren't, and people had. With every day, week, month and year, things seemed only to be getting worse.

Elsewhere, within the various bureaucracies, there was a kind of receptive wariness. There was an acknowledgement of the merits of the argument, but the cost and complexity actually doing something about it seemed too much. It was Maslow's hammer at work again: the kind of problems that I had observed and catalogued were not of the kind that anyone had trained for. The solutions and suggestions that I offered were not within anyone's powers or pay grade.

Cultural leaders who worked in funded galleries or administered top-down programs didn't see themselves as fostering small businesses and enterprise. Planners were looking at problems of a totally different nature and on a totally different scale. Economic development struggled with the reality, which I freely acknowledged, that a lot of what I wanted to encourage would at best be a marginal economic proposition. They wanted to see business plans before they would consider assisting anyone.

The formal processes were tiring. It was almost as though they were designed to involve the maximum amount of effort—meetings, follow-up, requests for information—to produce the minimum amount of action. I began to suspect it was a road with thousands of unexpected twists and turns, designed primarily to conceal the fact that it led to a dead end.

I am not a patient person. Perhaps if I was still living in Newcastle I might have felt more inclined to pressure and persevere. Perhaps that is why it worked this time and hadn't before. My time and travel was expensive. I watched my bank balance depleting with every trip for every pointless meeting. If anything was going to happen before I ran out of time and money, it wasn't going to come by working this way.

It wasn't practically possible to change the political culture with the resources I had at hand. I briefly contemplated a tilt at local politics before it dawned on me that if I did, not only would everything become counterproductively politicised, but my life would become a constant stream of these frustrations and pointless meetings.

It was illustrative, and perversely, inspiring. Gratuitous complexity was the very opposite of what we needed to encourage. Everything had to be made easier. It had to make sense from the bottom up. It had to be designed from the user's point of view. We needed to make the byzantine complexity of all this just—go away.

We were not going to get the city council, the state government, and the federal government to work together to change their systems any time soon. We would have to invent some systems of our own. After months of running round in circles I began to realise that running around in circles was the very thing we needed to do away with.

I still have ambitions that can only be achieved through the political system. But changing the way the city and the country works in a formal sense has drifted to the backburner. If anything in Newcastle was going to change at a pace I could afford to be involved with, it would have to happen another way.

We needed not so much to change the core way the city worked, but to find as many ways as we could to get around it. As others would later describe it, we needed not so much to change the city's systems as to hack them.

Chapter Eleven—

A LONG LAUNCH

I've lost track of my trips up to Newcastle. At one point, I counted more than forty of them. Now they all tend to blur together. I got to know a lot about pub accommodation, cheap hotels, and friends' floors. I tied some visits in with work trips to Sydney, and worked others around bargain airline sales, trying (and failing) not to burn through my savings.

I often travelled alone. My partner Narinda came with me when she could, and fortunately she was extraordinarily supportive of what was an increasingly crazy commitment. At times her skills were indispensable. It was her photos of Newcastle's empty buildings that became the 'before' shots that have been reproduced often since. She built the Renew Newcastle website.

Momentum is a strange thing. It always seemed like it was about to peter out, but little things kept happening that encouraged me to go back just one more time. Rod would discover something. There would be a potential lead about a property owner. Someone significant would agree to meet. At one low ebb, I looked again at the Facebook group that I had founded for the Renew Newcastle idea, and realised it had been growing exponentially. Thousands of members and well-wishers made me feel like I should probably keep going.

At a crucial moment, The Lock Up, a cultural centre and museum in the city's former police station, offered me a bed and a venue. They had two separate one-week gaps in their artist-in-residency program a few weeks apart in August and September of 2008. They offered me a room to sleep in, and the use of a former prison exercise yard as a venue. I put those dates in my diary as a self-imposed deadline.

I asked Craig to speak at a public meeting and hoped I could get enough of a plan together that I wouldn't be embarrassed talking publicly about it. Alone in that tiny apartment I watched Usain Bolt win the hundred-metres in Beijing and wondered how I would ever extricate myself from this mess of half-formed ideas and rising expectations that I found myself in.

On the 20th of August, my former colleagues at 1233 ABC Newcastle coaxed me onto morning radio. For the first time I told their listeners, the public, what I was planning to do. I was still making it up. Reading back their news summary of that interview, I was probably only about halfway there:

> Vacant shopfronts in the Newcastle CBD should be opened up to community arts and not-for-profit groups, under control of a property trust that assists building owners with tax concessions.

I went on to explain that Newcastle couldn't wait.

> There's been a long-term (trend) of deferring the future, of just

> imagining that in five or ten years or fifteen years from now that we'll redevelop that site or something will happen and that's when we'll fix things up . . . In between times . . . there are literally buildings that are being left to rot . . . at least a hundred empty shops (in Hunter St).

I tried to sound confident, but looking back there were still many unknowns. There were pieces I hadn't figured out, and problems I hadn't solved. Questions I hadn't answered. Things I was bullshitting my way through in the hope I could figure out an answer—or find someone who could—before anyone asked.

> Mr Westbury says a trust "will provide a healthy tax concession" as well as basic maintenance as well as short- or long-term tenants. And it would not involve large outlays of money. "One of the aims of this project is to come up with a strategy that isn't very expensive," he says. "A trust needs to have a small staff and be able to broker relationships with people . . . being able to marshal initiatives within the local community."
>
> He said providing tangible solution for building owners will be the key to the success of such a scheme, rather than relying on the goodwill of property owners. "Relying on goodwill isn't actually a strategy," Mr Westbury said. "The strategy I think is to offer the owners something that actually solves a problem for them, and the fact that their buildings are falling apart and decaying, losing value and generating bad will. Driving down property prices doesn't actually help them."

In that interview I relied a lot on the idea of tax concessions. I don't really remember whether I actually thought it was going to work like that or not. Perhaps I thought I could prompt government into action by suggesting they needed to provide that kick. Perhaps I was just seeding the idea of vital tax concessions as my exit strategy for if and when it all went pear-shaped. As it transpired, there never were any tax concessions but it didn't matter. The word 'trust' ultimately proved legally incorrect but the rest of it, for the most part, was a fair description of the plan.

A few weeks later on a Wednesday night in early September, Newcastle's former police station's prison exercise yard was full to overflowing. 'The room was packed, every seat taken and dozens of people sitting cross-legged on scraps of carpet and bare concrete,' according to the press reports. They didn't mention that I was nervously clutching a longneck of beer in a brown paper bag from the bottle shop across the road as Craig Allchin began telling stories and showing pictures of the transformation of Melbourne on a slightly misaligned video projector.

That night has been mythologised and misremembered on more than a few occasions since. I have probably been responsible for more than a few different versions. But Lisa Pryor, a columnist with the *Sydney Morning Herald*, was there and recorded a reliable account in following Saturday's paper. She said of the city,

> Hunter Street, once the main shopping strip of the central business district, is falling apart. Too long and particularly inconvenient in this era of suburban shopping malls, the street has become a string of empty shopfronts, interrupted by retail non sequiturs: a tattoo parlour, a theatre, car dealerships, a scrapbooking shop.

She went on to summarise the plan as presented on the night.

> Because this is Newcastle, not Sydney, Westbury's plan for renewal is cheaper and more lateral than granite paving, steel and glass. The creative communities of the town might not have the capital, but they do have "sweat equity" or elbow grease. So he proposes putting artists and fashion designers, community groups and musicians, into those empty buildings, to use and maintain them while they are awaiting redevelopment.

> Before you think this is all pie-in-the-sky hippy stuff, here are the details. The plan will be administered through a trust, which is adequately financed and insured, led by a board including representatives from government, the law and the arts. This way property owners can feel confident lending their properties for short-term management and custodianship, knowing a bunch of crazy artists aren't going to smash it to bits or refuse to leave when the time comes. If they do, the trust will be responsible.

Pryor, for her part, seemed more convinced than I was. Newcastle, she said, was 'a place where it is not only possible but affordable to live within walking distance of beach and city,' which 'provides a genuine alternative for those who love the urban feel of Sydney but don't like its expense.' By the end of her article she was suggesting to her Sydney-based readers, 'Let's all move there.'

It was a positive view of the city, its assets and its obvious potential. It was an upbeat assessment only made remarkable by the fact that such optimism was rare. It ran counter to the usual predictions of doom and gloom.

The significance of that night wasn't in anything I said, or even in what Craig said. It was actually in the audience. Dotted throughout the crowded room were the people with the missing pieces of the puzzle, people I had been trying and failing to meet with, who did indeed have ideas for projects in those empty buildings.

There were significant business and community leaders in attendance, people who would go on to become Renew Newcastle's champions, board members and leaders and people who held the keys to dozens of empty properties in the city.

A few rows back was the person who would soon become the most important person of all. Marni Jackson was in the final weeks of preparation for October's This Is Not Art festival. She was the festival manager responsible for the logistics of the event. I had gotten to know her two years beforehand, when she had asked me to help salvage the National Young Writers Festival which had dramatically imploded.

It had lost its directors about six weeks before the program was due. I helped her put a program together as we recruited new directors, and hastily put the festival back on an even keel. How people cope under pressure shows you the best and worst of them. In that chaos, I saw one of the most impressive, indefatigable, levelheaded, hard-working, empathetic, organised and brilliant people I'd ever had the pleasure to work with.

I'd already decided that Marni was the best and the most obvious person to actually run whatever this thing was going to be...I just hadn't told her yet. I made the strategic decision not hassle her about details six weeks out from the festival, but I did my best to subtly get her involved.

When the paperwork was required to register the not-for-profit company, we needed at least three founding directors. I asked Marni if she'd mind lending her name to a bit of paperwork. I told her she could always back out later. The founding directors of Renew Newcastle were Craig, Marni and myself.

As Marni's festival role wound up, she gradually became the eyes and ears of Renew Newcastle—reducing the need for me to go back and forth for every little thing. She quickly became its heart, its muscle, and most of its brain as well. The following year she became its first employee.

Marni had the perfect combination of skills and temperament for the role. She could talk to a property owner or a struggling artist. She could see and balance multiple different perspectives on complex issues. She had grace under fire and a quiet and resolute confidence that made people believe in her. I believed in her. She knew what she knew and what she didn't.

In the first year or so of Renew Newcastle, Marni would ring me regularly for advice and reassurance. In the years that have followed I came to mostly ring her for the same reasons.

Further up the back of that prison exercise yard listening quietly was someone who, had I realised they were there, would have made me a little more discreet about the beer in my brown paper bag. David Sleet was the manager of a proposed bricks-and-mortar revitalisation of the city centre for the GPT Group—one of Australia's largest property companies. The company had quietly been acquiring city blocks around the Hunter Street Mall for several years.

At that time, they were proposing a large retail development on the site, and their ambitions were the talk of the city. In the years that would follow, the story of GPT's development in Newcastle became increasingly complicated. It is a saga with so many twists and turns it is probably worthy of a miniseries. But in 2008, on the eve of the Global Financial Crisis, they were proposing a half-billion-dollar development that would transform central Newcastle.

They thought it was a couple of years away, and so were laying the groundwork, floating designs, consulting with the community and seeking various concessions from government. They were mindful that they needed community support to do what they had proposed.

They also had a more immediate dilemma. In the process of buying up properties, they had, with no particular intent, made the vacancy situation worse. Owner-occupiers had been bought out. Long-term tenants had moved on as their future was made uncertain by the pending development.

As David would explain in a 2010 interview with the Empty Spaces Project at the University of Technology, Sydney:

> We knew that there was a period before GPT's Newcastle CBD development would commence and as a result, we were focussed on developing strategies to reactivate the mall... We had a number of vacant properties for lease, some of which were difficult to lease due to their locations and/or format. These properties were offered to Renew Newcastle.

They were an ideal first partner. They had scale. Even their 'difficult to lease' properties amounted to a quantity of sites that I hadn't imagined having access to any time soon. The fact that they were a risk-averse multinational-listed company was a good thing. They weren't the types to allow us to gloss over the details or fudge things with a handshake deal.

> At the outset, we were unsure about the longevity and sustainability of participants in the scheme... Would the businesses be open and for how long? What improvements to the properties would we need to make and at what cost? Who maintains the upkeep of the properties? Who pays running costs? What about breakages and shop-front vandalism? Will we have ongoing issues if a retail tenant becomes available on a commercial arrangement? We considered the impact on possible commercial agreements and running costs, along with general legal issues and planning approvals.

Their concerns were mostly the ones we had already planned for, but they forced us to formalise them. Within weeks I was shuttling back and forth between meetings in Newcastle, Sydney, and Melbourne to iron out the terms and conditions.

That we had dotted our i's and crossed our t's meant that

those discussions progressed quickly. Striking the right balance between thoroughness and simplicity, the arrangement drawn up between Rod, his colleagues at Sparke Helmore, and the GPT legal team became a template for a model that would go on to unlock vacant properties for hundreds of creative projects and businesses around Australia.

GPT were the ideal partner for another reason. David got it. I don't know when or where or how he was converted. Whether he was impressed by that prison presentation, whether we helped reinforce what he believed anyway, or whether he was simply convinced by the results, he became an ally and advocate. He offered his time to the project out of work hours. He helped us well beyond the description of his day job even after his involvement in Newcastle ended.

He would tell me later that he enjoyed coming to Newcastle because it was the only place in the country where he could pick up a present for his kids that was made there.

Just days before Christmas 2008, Marni and I sat down with David and signed a peppercorn agreement. I gave them a dollar from my own pocket and they gave us the keys to about a dozen properties. It had been a year and a half since I'd sat down to write about Newcastle, about ten months since the article appeared in *Griffith REVIEW*, about six months since that fateful beer with Craig, and four months from the first meeting with Rod.

We opened our call for proposals at the worst possible time, at a time that is, for most Australians, the beginning of a six-week summer holiday break when retail spending slumps, families go away, and most people generally enjoy not having to think at all about what might occupy them in the new year.

We had secured more spaces than I had dreamed of, but many were GPTs 'difficult to lease' sites for a reason. They deliberately held back the properties they had commercial interest in and thought they could rent soon.

It was a beautiful and terrifying moment. I had been blindly reassuring the property owners and the business community there was no lack of creative, enthusiastic ideas in the city, but in the absence of any actual buildings I had only been talking in quite general terms. Many of the artists I'd met with had impractical and (occasionally) harebrained ideas about what it was that they proposed to do. There was little guarantee that the practical constraints that we were operating in and the passions of the community would actually meet in the middle.

I was having a Wile E. Coyote moment. In the blitz of activity and momentum that had sustained the idea to that point, I may well have run straight off a cliff. We still didn't have any money. We couldn't pay anyone. Partially out of uncertainty, partially out of fear of accusations of nepotism and cronyism, I had deliberately avoided speculating about who the end users would be, even to myself. I didn't have a single concrete example of anyone who actually wanted to, and more importantly, was able to move into a space yet.

We had no money for marketing or advertising. We had no budget for capital works. We didn't print a single poster. We didn't have a marketing or PR person. We didn't have any paid staff at all and I didn't even live in town—it was costing me hundreds of dollars every time I had to come up and meet someone.

Instead, we relied heavily on our Facebook group and its two- or three-thousand members. We generated a few stories in the local press. We built networks through the local Olive

Tree design markets; I spoke to tutors at the University and individually emailed Newcastle-based Etsy stores.

Eventually the hastily-cobbled-together Gmail account we used for project submissions began to fill up. Soon it had grown into ten, then twenty, then thirty and forty project proposals. At the beginning of 2009 it looked as though we might actually be onto something.

Chapter Twelve—

THE POETRY OF CONSTRAINT

Ingenuity and desperation can be the best form of innovation. Renew Newcastle was the culmination of all that thinking, prodding, begging, observing, despairing and doing. Legally it is not a 'trust' but a not-for-profit company limited by guarantee. It is an arts organisation, in the broadest sense of the term.

Today if you give us money, it is the equivalent of a donation to charity. We are a tax-deductible cultural organisation, but we never did change the property laws. Lending us property has never been tax-deductible or eligible for any kind of tax or rate refund.

In the early days Renew Newcastle didn't have an office—it had a PO Box. It mostly existed in the ether. Its first manifestation was a Facebook page. It lived for a while between Rod's office, Marni's and my mobile phones, and a shared email address. As the project took off, it took up residence in a building we borrowed from GPT.

St Mark's was a dark-brown early '80s-era Catholic church just off Hunter Street. It still had the Stations of The Cross around the brown brick walls, an old photo of John Paul II, and three functioning confession booths complete with a noisy buzzer to summon the priests.

We salvaged an old letterboard sign and proclaimed the venue the Ann Foat Hall in mismatched fonts. The name was in honour of our first benefactor, who had written us a cheque for five hundred dollars on the back of that first public meeting. The cheque sat on a desk for a month or more because we didn't have a bank account.

We had moved into the church because we assumed, wrongly as it turned out, that it was the least likely building to rent out. When a church group came looking for a venue we, like many of our projects before and since, found ourselves on the move to a nondescript single room office above the Hunter Street Mall. Both offices were adorned with a collection of kitsch amateur op-shop tapestries of pets and landscapes that Marni gradually accumulated.

The name was an afterthought. When it was going to be a 'trust' the idea of a 'Renewal Trust' sounded sufficiently respectable that property owners might lend their properties to it. I'd always liked 'renewal' as a concept but that had largely been in another context. In my other life I'd never had to think about all the connotations that 'urban renewal' had had loaded upon it by government schemes and the property industry.

'Renew Newcastle' arose by default. It felt clumsy but I liked the repetition of 'new New' in the middle. I thought we could use 'new New' for an event, or as a design feature or a campaign of some kind. We never did.

We began with the big problem: how much spaces cost and the terms they were available on. Most of the reasons these spaces sat empty were medium-term ones—the limbo created by the uncertainty of what would happen next. We designed a system for limbo. Festivals had taught me that the hardest part was not getting the owner to let you have a building, but getting them to let you have a building at some future date—in October or May or at whenever you would need it.

More often than not the owner didn't know what they would be doing then. So a Renew project ideally would begin tomorrow and continue on a rolling thirty-day agreement, indefinitely into the future. It would last until it converted to a conventional lease, the project ended, or the owner needed the building back. For some buildings that ended up being thirty days, but for one it is now six years and counting.

That was the basic premise of the system. Our projects would be planted until the property was needed again, but would have no security. If they needed security, they would need to pay rent. They or we would pay whatever costs incurred by them being there: gas, water, electricity and any other costs or fees that the owner incurred for their presence. We wouldn't contribute to the holding costs of the property except by virtue of a practical contribution in kind.

Written into agreements were obligations and expectations. We would clean up spaces. We would ensure they were open at mutually agreed-upon times. Those times would depend on if the site was a shop or an office, or on the expectations of the location. We would often do minor maintenance such as repairing broken glass, painting properties, and other things that can be achieved through sweat and a working bee.

As we became more confident and ambitious, we began to do other minor works. We installed emergency exit lights, checked and reconnected power, and removed rubbish and debris in exchange for access to properties.

I learned more than I had ever intended to know about property law. For one thing, I learned the difference between a license and a lease. We didn't need or *want* a lease. For our purposes we did not need to take 'possession,' merely to allow someone to go in and out at particular times for particular purposes.

Retail leases in particular place a high burden on the owner. By default, they confer long-term rights designed to stop unscrupulous owners throwing out successful businesses and replacing them with ones run by their cousins. These could be waived, but you needed to declare that you had your own legal advice and understood the consequences. As many of our projects didn't have a lawyer, we found them one. A simple template form and quick consultation with a local community legal centre turned that burden into a streamlined and simple process.

We neither wanted nor needed the security of tenure. We wanted to try things. We didn't want to place upon the owners the responsibility that comes by default with a commercial property lease or a retail tenancy. We would try not to hassle the owner about the small things. If the hot water stopped working, we would try to deal with it ourselves. If it hadn't worked in years, we would find a project that didn't need it. In exchange for free access to empty properties, no one was surprised they wouldn't be getting all the bells and whistles.

We didn't need to take buildings out of the rental market

in order to be able to use them. It made no difference that the building might still be for lease beyond the awkward aesthetics of where to put any 'For Lease' signs. In the internet age, we discovered that signs are mostly redundant anyway, and a strip full of competing giant 'No One Is Here' signs are the opposite of appealing to potential investors.

Beyond some simple practicalities, there was no problem with the agent continuing to advertise the property and the owner continuing to show prospective tenants through. The fact that someone was there keeping them open actually made properties easier to casually inspect. If the trade-off was that we could get the space cheaply and easily and make it active, then all the better. "While we are waiting" can be a very long time.

We also recognised that in order to be able to do something temporarily, the owner needed to be convinced that it really *would* be temporary. For a lot of owners, the biggest fear was not in letting us have the building—after all, it would cost them nothing and potentially grow value and interest—but that when they needed it, they might not get the building back. The last thing that we or they wanted to see was a front-page story in a local newspaper screaming, 'Evil property owner throws out much-loved community project!' when in fact the owner may well be indirectly responsible for the very existence of that project in the first place.

We had to establish very clearly from the beginning that Renew Newcastle was not only there to manage getting people into empty buildings, but *also* to manage getting them out. We set those expectations transparently and clearly among the projects from the very beginning. We knew our ability to secure properties in future would depend on it.

If our projects wanted security, in most cases there would be nothing to stop them signing a commercial lease and making a long-term commitment—but that wasn't our job. I liked to remind people that if that didn't happen they would inevitably, eventually get kicked out.

Somewhere in the mess of paperwork and advice, observations and conversations, I discovered something completely counterintuitive. It turned out it was actually easier to borrow an empty building than it was to cheaply rent one.

Part of that was opportunity cost. The other part was to do with all that stuff about banks and solvency and leverage. We heard from more than one owner that the fact that the property was not leased and remained on the market meant the financial implications of writing down the rent were never triggered.

In keeping with our idea of letting projects be driven by artists themselves, we realised that the role of Renew is really as a 'process shepherd.' We made it our role to find people to help, and stepped them deftly around the roadblocks and complexities that might otherwise have been in their way.

Our job was to work out what can be made easy—what people could do cheaply and what they couldn't. Such a simple thing, but no one in Newcastle or in most other places had ever done this, as far as I could tell.

I'd learned that most of the legal complexities that got in the way of small projects were triggered by a change of use for a building. But no permit has ever been required to use a shop as a shop, or an office as an office. The complexities are introduced when you try to convert a shop to a restaurant, an office to a performance space, or anything else that takes a building out of the category it is already approved for. So, for the most part, we didn't.

We lowered our expectations. That was a good thing. Rather than look for the best possible or most profitable use of any given space, we looked for the best practical use. That is a simple distinction, but one with many consequences. Often the best possible use would require a major renovation, long planning processes, and an indefinite period of uncertainty. The most profitable one could likely be years away. Our role was to do something while all that was happening.

We aimed for the projects that were ready to go immediately and that were consistent with what the existing permissions said you could do. On the downside, some of the best proposals we received—for cinemas and performance venues, for projects involving booze and food and crowds—were for things we never did. On the upside, we have done a lot more than any organisation with similar resources should ever have been able to do.

Where necessary, we asked forgiveness, not permission. We didn't have time to wait for processes to click into gear. Instead we got good advice both from within and outside of government about our rights, and set about asserting them. In an adversarial legal system there is a massive difference between someone who asks, *What am I allowed to do?* and someone who asserts their right to do it. The latter has always been the privilege of those with capital, and rarely of the under-resourced. In any case, the risk of being shut down on a technicality was low as long as you didn't overcapitalise and could move on cheaply—two things that for us were necessary anyway.

For individual projects, we helped manage the nuances of their proposals. We guided our projects through trigger points and around key words lest they invoke the wrath of unnecessary complication. As a simple example, there are several different definitions of a 'gallery' for planning purposes: one is a shop that sells art, and the other is a public institution and place of assembly with all the extra issues involved. All our galleries were shops that sold artwork, and we never allowed a planner or regulatory authority to assume otherwise.

Where possible, we encouraged people to tweak the more complicated aspects of their otherwise simple proposals. Complex equipment onsite or issues around alcohol, performance, food and beverages would often be deferred to a later stage in the interests of getting things in immediately. We also realised the need to manage ambiguities. A shop where you do some sewing would be okay. A factory where you made clothing would not. In practice, the difference was often as simple as who you asked and how you talked about it.

There were some simple practical challenges for many small businesspeople and creative groups in being expected to operate as a month-by-month proposition. Services were difficult to get connected for a month at a time. We ad-libbed that as we went, and generally erred towards doing it however was simplest.

Electricity and gas were not always easy to connect upfront. In some cases the projects dealt with it; sometimes we put them in our own name. Other times, we left them in the owner's name and agreed to be a guarantor and manage the payment process.

Internet access was initially a problem. In the early stages it could only be secured on long contracts or with big upfront fees. For many of our projects, the internet was their primary place of business. Over a six-pack of beer on the steps of the church, Chris Deere—the founder of Ipera, a locally owned

Internet Service Provider—and I sketched out a plan to set up wifi around the entire precinct.

We killed two birds with one stone, by providing a limited free wifi service to the public and a free business-grade service to new projects that were casually filling many spaces nearby. Over time, the emergence of public hotspots and competitively priced 3G and 4G data services made that hurdle largely disappear.

The last, and most expensive, if not the trickiest piece of the puzzle was insurance. We couldn't avoid it. Public liability insurance and insurance against damage to property were legal necessities. Yet such policies were often only available on an annual basis, for very specific kinds of initiatives (market stallholders or exhibiting artists can access more casual policies than shop owners, for example), or came with an extremely high premium for short-term projects.

We solved this problem in a simple and obvious way. The local business traders association paid upfront for that first policy, and today we operate an umbrella policy for all our projects. We provide access to it for a small weekly fee for each participant.

Few, if any, of these solutions were novel in and of themselves. Collectively, they added up to a whole new system—a system for catalysing, managing, and enabling a whole new layer of activity in the city. We had stepped around the default legal framework within which most property in Australia is managed, and created a new one in its cracks.

We created new rules, new contracts and new conditions. We hacked them together from precedents that covered mobile phone towers and billboards, from observations of and conversations with property insiders, from microfinance, from community activism, and from other arts services and *pro bono* organisations.

Our system was designed to make the city work for people for whom it had not worked in a long time. Our stakeholders were people without capital, for whom barriers to entry, and not certainty or security of outcome were the defining challenge. Digital cottage industries. Online artisans. Artists and fashion designers with market stalls. Bedroom record labels. Flickr photographers. Community groups.

It had taken every lesson I had ever learned, every brain I had ever picked, and every ally I could possibly find. We tried to make physical spaces behave with as much simplicity as virtual spaces did, and built a whole suite of tools and structures and plug-ins. It was a complex system designed to create simplicity—a system that would make as much of everyone else's complexity and risk into our problem as it possibly could.

Part Four—

MAKING CHANGE

Chapter Thirteen—

KEYS TO THE CITY

Across the road from Newcastle's still-decaying Post Office, on the first floor of a 19th Century bank building, you will find a little group of technology, media, and design offices. From their window you could almost throw a stone onto the roof of that prison yard where that first public meeting about Renew Newcastle was held.

Neither Zac Zavos, who runs Conversant Media, an online publishing company, nor Abby Farmer and Clare Gleeson, who run the design studio Neon Zoo, are still part of the Renew Newcastle program. They moved out of their borrowed offices in search of more space and more certainty several years ago. The other businesses that have clustered around them and the wine bar downstairs aren't part of Renew Newcastle either. But it is difficult to imagine how much, if any, of this would be there had it never existed.

Neon Zoo and Conversant Media share not just an office

but a particular part of this history. They were there at the very beginning, in late 2008, when both businesses were run from home. Their businesses were small. Their talents were obvious. But like many small businesses, they were uncertain about what risks to take and what moves to make in order to grow.

Abby, Clare and Zac were amongst ten or fifteen people who toured an odd collection of empty shops and offices on a hot summer afternoon. GPT had lent Marni and me a pile of keys to a group of those 'difficult to lease,' unloved, and unwanted spaces. They included the old church that would soon become Renew's offices, an abandoned '50s-era former ophthalmology surgery on the hill above, and a small collection of empty main-street former fashion and retail stores. Some had only recently been vacated while others had been empty for as long as I could remember. One small group of properties had been redeveloped nearly a decade earlier and had literally never had a tenant.

Today Zac's business, Conversant Media, has a team of ten people. They support 75 paid contributors including some of Australia's best-known sports, culture and technology writers. They have an investment from Network Ten—one of Australia's major television networks—and millions of dollars in revenue. Their websites include the culture site Lost At E Minor, sports opinion site The Roar, and technology site Techly, which collectively attract two-and-a-half million viewers a month and reach more than five million people on Facebook.

Six years ago it was a different story. Zac was in the crowd at that first fateful meeting, with his brother and business partner Zolton on the other side of the world in the United States. He was working alone from home with a young family and struggling. "To be honest, it was the hardest period of my life. I'd given up a lot to do it and there are moments I remember very well of feeling I was in a corner, and I couldn't get out," he would later tell the *Newcastle Herald*.

On a similar journey, if not in the same dire state, were Abby and Clare, fellow designers Tim Neve and Heath Killen, stop motion animator Jane Shadbolt and filmmaker Stuart McBratney. Photographers Daniel Danuser and Mark St Clair dreamed of opening a dedicated photography space, Gallery Raw, for the burgeoning community of photographers that was growing around Newcastle and in many other places at that time.

In the 1970s Mark had worked on the same strip as a window dresser. By 2008 the David Jones department store where Mark had begun his working life was in its death throes. It would soon announce its closure and disappear for good. As we walked, he reminisced that once, "You couldn't walk down this part of Hunter Street at peak hour because there were too many people." Apart from us, there was virtually no one.

Damian Castaldi and Solange Kershaw were media artists, part-time university teachers and relatively recent arrivals to Newcastle. They planned to establish Newcastle's (and probably Australia's) only dedicated sound art gallery. They proposed 'a commercial gallery for exhibition of sound and interactive media works featuring local and national sound artists, sound sculptors and digital/interactive media artists.' They took a particular liking to a discarded menswear store because the empty change rooms would make great listening booths for audio art.

Emma Stronach's Emerald Arts was to be a place where she would make and sell her own handmade toys, books, and prints. She would make educational art and craft kits and run classes for children. Edwina Richards also had craft-based ambitions. She was part of a fledgling group of local artisans and makers called Make Space.

Later she would describe the experience of "looking at the massive bunch of 'keys to the city' ... thinking 'is this a dream?'" To her, "The idea of Renew was so revolutionary and embryonic at the time that I had an uncertain few weeks of 'is it too good to be true?'" She was so sceptical that it took "a meeting with a lawyer friend for me to realise that it was both true and too good to pass up."

Despite Newcastle being a relatively small city, with what seemed to be a small creative community, most of the people on our first property tour had never met each other. It was the first time that I had met most of them. I knew two of them casually, but none of them well. They came from a range of ages—from barely out of their teens to pushing towards retirement—and had arrived via different trajectories. Some had business plans. Others were pure art-for-arts-sake, while others were primarily concerned with building a likeminded community.

They weren't part of any one particular group, business network or social scene. They had come from established families, in the area for generations, or had only recently moved to Newcastle for work or for love; a few had lived away and returned with a fresh sense of what the city could and should be.

Despite my initial fears that no one would apply, the hard part had actually been whittling the applicants down. I recently dug out an old spreadsheet that listed the first eleven successful proposals by their application numbers. The successful ones are numbered between 19 and 86. There were twenty or thirty more that would have been worth doing and viable if the right spaces had been available. Another third had obvious potential.

Many of those would later go on to refine their projects and establish themselves as the program grew, brought on more properties, and found its feet. Inevitably some were, for one reason or another, not projects that would have been have practical. A few were downright scary, and a couple were probably bordering on illegal.

Looking back, that first group was a more risk-averse selection than some that would follow. The successful applicants were, on average, a little more experienced than some we would later go on to support. We deliberately chose carefully and somewhat conservatively, with our main criterion being that none of them would do anything that would screw it all up. Yet even with that constraint, they collectively demonstrated the diversity of pent-up demand in the city.

In the mad few weeks that followed, Marni and I began to match them up not only to spaces, but to each other. The problematic old eye doctor's surgery at the top of the hill was soon transformed into what its tenants decided to call The Clinic. Zac, Abby, Clare, the other designers, and Stuart the filmmaker moved in. The rabbit warren of individual consulting spaces, most still complete with eye charts, began to fill with what had once been mostly home-based laptop businesses. It became an instant and largely self-organising incubator.

The very action of bringing these people into proximity with each other soon began to yield results. People who had never met become each other's collaborators and contributors. "Having that space with other, I guess, like-minded or interested people was so important," Zac Zavos would later say:

> We referred work to Neon Zoo, they referred work to us, Heath [Killen] did our design, and all of this was business that wouldn't otherwise have happened. Moving from my sunroom to an office space which had been otherwise empty had an enormous impact on my business. It meant I could meet clients, and hire people, earlier than I otherwise would ... There's something about having a space for business. You'd have meetings more readily with good people and the most important thing was that people knew they could just drop in.

In the years since many more businesses have crossed paths as they passed through The Clinic and other similar spaces. Like Neon Zoo and Conversant Media, when it came time to grow they often ended up moving out, onwards and upwards, together.

Down the hill, in the shops that would face the public, there was a frenzy of cleaning and preparation. Edwina and the four other people initially behind Make Space spent a week pulling up carpets, painting, and making shelving. Make Space had no ambitions to be a big business. It was a community project, and one that ultimately lasted five years across five separate properties.

They moved from borrowed space to borrowed space. They made do with discarded furniture from hard rubbish collections and white paint mixed from half-used cans from family garages and garden sheds. Each time they moved they made the places they moved to and the places around them better.

Make Space spent just $300 fitting out its first site. They later boasted that they never spent more than $50 on any subsequent space. One move and makeover cost just 50 cents. "We reused and recycled everything," Edwina proudly proclaimed.

Despite, or perhaps because of that, one visual merchandiser I know of gleaned a list of ideas from them for projects with budgets ten, a hundred or even a thousand times higher.

I had talked a lot about 'sweat equity' as I was talking up the idea of Renew. I hadn't realised how literal that would be. That January was hot. Moving in was hard work. Temperatures peaked well above 40°C. Often air conditioning was on the 'things we have to do without' list.

At Loop Space, the sound art gallery, Damien, in his singlet with a broom and power tools, become an iconic image of the early days of the project. He and Solange were hammering, cleaning, sweeping, painting, scrounging, preparing and presenting their space. Jane Shadbolt moved her tiny animation studio upstairs.

Next door to them, Kim Bridgland, Ksenia Totoeva, and a group of young architecture students were stripping back decades of bad retail fittings, fake ceilings and ugly veneers to reveal the hidden beauty of hundred-year-old ceiling beams. They made a stunning architectural intervention as they cut literally thousands of wood blocks to form an undulating topographical floor to cover the sterile white tiles of an empty former sandwich bar.

Those first projects were beginning a process that would be repeated more than a hundred times. Their trajectories are a little snapshot of where those seeds that were being planted could lead.

Some, like Conversant Media and Neon Zoo, provide a straight and simple business incubation success story. They built businesses which employed people. They created jobs. It is the kind of impact that is beloved by bean counters, and civic and political leaders. It's a simple story, and a genuinely good one. It is one that is easy to measure and easy to tell.

Others succeeded in other ways. Some projects were only meant to be temporary. The architecture students came and went, leaving behind a much-improved space for an early Renew retailer who would later sign a commercial lease to move in a few months later. Some failed cheaply but mostly fruitfully in some way or other. No one had to lose their house to discover that they'd failed.

Emerald Arts was eventually forced out, not by a commercial tenant, but by a series of rainstorms. Emma's building leaked badly and was too far gone to hold up without significant repairs, which none of us could afford.

Loop Space, the sound art gallery, lasted more than a year, but never did become commercially sustainable. Despite the proposal for a 'commercial gallery,' in practice art, not commerce, was the prevailing purpose. Damien and Solange moved on to new ideas and new projects. By the time they did, they had hosted many of Australia's leading sound and media artists and showcased international artists of the calibre of Laurie Anderson.

Gallery Raw lasted a couple of years in two locations. It nurtured the careers of dozens of local photographers. It inspired and introduced to the city other photographers. Some of them would go on to become some of the most successful participants in Renew. It catalysed a community of friends, colleagues, and photography lovers.

Some of those early opening nights attracted so many people that it must have, at least for a moment, reminded Mark of those better, younger days. The first time I had seen a crowd in the mall in years was watching people spill over onto the footpaths and bustling for their chance to get into one particularly successful group photography show.

By the time Make Space wound up nearly five years later more than seventy local artisans had been represented there. It would have been the first retail stockist for many of them. It was a chance for many to grow their own skills, careers, businesses, spaces and labels.

Some of the makers they stocked graduated to having their own spaces, through Renew and commercially. Meanwhile, I lost count of the number of times that the various Make Space offshoots featured in travel features and lists of 'must visit' highlights of things to do in Newcastle.

But the process that had begun was not just about the projects. It was about the city. Something had begun to change in the psyche of the place. For the first time in years, the number of vacancies in Newcastle began going down rather than up. Shops were opening, rather than closing. As global events and political shenanigans began to unravel yet another of the city's big-picture plans, the streets were beginning to gleam with little shards of hope and opportunity.

Amy De Lore, the editor of the *Newcastle Herald's* weekend magazine, celebrated Christmas 2009 with a snapshot of the city as she had seen it change from twelve months before. A year before, she had left a group of five- and six-year-olds getting class photos with Santa Claus to walk back to her office.

As she passed along the mall where she once gone regularly for lunch, she despaired. She counted twelve or thirteen of twenty empty shops along that strip, before encountering what she vividly described as 'the sickeningly unmistakable thud of a clenched fist meeting a cheekbone' as a violent altercation broke out in front of her.

She had despaired at the 'parlous decay,' the 'depressingly empty shopfronts,' the graffiti and the broken windows and the experience of feeling 'like and extra in some B-grade movie about the Apocalypse.'

> [J]ust one year later there is a much more encouraging column to be written ... I walked down the mall again this week and the change in it since December 2008 is nothing short of outstanding. Some of the small galleries have evolved into viable retail shops ... retailers seem to be rediscovering the precinct... the slide has not only been arrested but turned around.

That same month another *Herald* article would declare the transformation 'the miracle on Hunter Street.'

Chapter Fourteen—

LEARNING BY DOING

The best thing I can say about my personal ability to predict what would and wouldn't work in Newcastle is that I learned very quickly not to even try.

Projects that I was convinced would be bulletproof often failed quickly. People who I had unwavering faith in sometimes gave up at the first setback. Yet for every one of those, there were people that I underestimated, projects I wrote off in advance as 'learning experiences,' markets for things I had barely realised existed, and communities for ideas that I'd never given a second thought to that also proved me wrong.

The goal was never to drag the entire city towards any 'vision' or any particular outcome. There was never a goal of where the project should end up or what the city should be. Renew was designed as a rejection of the single simple answer. What I *personally* liked was never the point of the exercise.

In this one key respect, my role at Renew was very different to anything I had done before. Working on festivals, making television, writing for newspapers and magazines had always, to some extent, been an extension of my own tastes, networks, interests and communities. This wasn't and shouldn't have been the case here.

Renew aimed to invert processes. It aimed to make what once had been hard easy, and what would once have been risky much less so. To take as much of what might once have been near impossible in the city and make it comparatively simple. The purpose was always to plant many seeds and see what grew. For that to work, the seeds couldn't all be the same. To nurture an ecology, you can't begin by planting a monoculture.

The point was never to fill the city with hipsters on fixed-gear bicycles, bearded designers, or trendy imports from somewhere else. The idea wasn't to turn the city over to the so-called 'creative class' or to attract star artists, cool brands or designers. Our concern was far more pragmatic and grounded. It was to ensure that lots of people in the Newcastle community could see themselves, their talents, their ideas and aspirations reflected in the city once more. For that to succeed, things would need to appeal to a far broader group than the tiny cohort of me.

In those early few months, Renew Newcastle had begun to create a Petri dish of preconditions that would attract people's initiative. The businesses and community projects that would take root in Newcastle would ultimately be a product of that low barrier to entry meeting the individual passions and initiative of hundreds of people.

The mix evolved as the project evolved, and the city evolved too. It changed with the mix of spaces available, and with each new example created by the success and failure of what had come before. Someone would open a shop, remake a property, or launch a business idea, and just by doing so, forge paths that others would be inspired and enabled to follow.

Some of it took some time to establish. Today there is a strong and growing mix of eclectic retailers in the city, and people have begun to think of the area as a retail destination again. But in those early stages, the lack of foot traffic was so dire that even our applicants were wary of retailing.

Within those first few years the Renew program supported teenagers designing skateboard decks and streetwear, and milliners who were making hats for people who may well have been their grandparents. A nineteen-year-old surf photographer named Alex Thompson's business Surfhouse Photography was the first to move out and into rent-paying premises.

While we put a strong premium on getting into empty shops and removing the symbols of decay, it was often the low-profile, hidden, and out-of-the-way spaces that were the better incubators. There was a certain freedom in starting a little bit off Broadway. There was less pressure in the spaces that no one particularly wanted, or was opinionated about.

As we grew more capable and more confident we took on more. By the time the David Jones department store left its central city location we had the skills, the means, and the confidence to convert the ground floor street frontage into The Emporium—home to a dozen maker-based artisanal businesses.

There was something strangely liberating about letting go of the illusion of control. Once you accept that you can't determine what will happen, it becomes much easier to discover what might. We deliberately tried different things and attempted to cross-pollinate ideas, businesses, artists, and audiences in the hope that serendipity and evolution would reveal what paths made sense. We aimed to find the shortest, cheapest, simplest and most efficient means to what other people could make work.

The projects that got access to the spaces were varied, but the process was always competitive. We learned from our mistakes. As we formalised our processes we managed to pare them down to a minimum series of practical requirements that would allow for a wide range of possibilities in practice. We looked for projects that knew their own audience and knew what they were trying to do. We resisted the urge to be all 'arts' or all 'business'. We looked for projects that had the potential to be viable on their own terms.

It wasn't for us to decide those terms, but if a project was to be volunteer-run we wanted to know if it had the volunteers. If it was a community project, did it represent the community it claimed to? If it was a business, was there reason to believe the person in charge could run it? And, of course, we needed to be confident that we could trust them with the space, that we could vouch for them to the property owners, and know that they would adhere to the responsibilities we had negotiated with and for them.

We were able to be guided, for better or for worse, by prioritising those things that we could make easy. We were always juggling two separate pools. On one hand we had whichever properties we could convince owners to make available to us, and on the other we had a broad and open call for project ideas. Each pool was being constantly refined, recast, and recalibrated as we went, and each one was informing the other.

While obviously not always ideal, the temporary nature of how projects began was often a liberation. It allowed us to take risks in a creative sense. We were not a government agency, though gradually we secured funding from state and local governments. We recognised that to do things we needed to take risks. We became a pro-risk organisation.

Risk, in this context, was a good thing. Our organisational culture was to always find reasons why we *could* do things, to find ways of doing them resourcefully, and not go looking for reasons why we might not. We looked for solutions, opportunities, and loopholes, and not reasons to be afraid.

Inevitably that means that we failed. We failed a *lot*. We were never to be defensive about failure. It was a cheap, controlled, and largely consequence-less failure, but it was still failure a lot of the time. Renew Newcastle tried many things that didn't work. More than half the things we have started aren't there anymore. We covered almost every letter of the alphabet, from artist studios to 'zine stores, and learned from the sheer diversity of it all.

The rule that we ultimately settled on was not that everyone must be an artist. People need not be young, or cool, or even see themselves as particularly 'creative'. But they must at least make what they do. We took a broad definition of that, but the rationale was as pragmatic as it was philosophical. That constraint had grown, as much as anything, from an obligation to the interests and concerns of the existing businesses in the city.

The need to 'make what you do' generally meant you weren't directly competing with an existing businesses—something that every Renew project explicitly couldn't do. Inevitably, that cut us off from many potentially sustainable businesses, and made it much harder to reach the volumes required for sustainability, but it was a fair trade-off and meant that everything was adding something different and unique to the mix.

Behind the scenes we worked within a series of often-invisible constraints. Often it was the properties themselves that settled who would be successful. While we may have had twenty applications to choose from, often only one or two of them made sense in a given space.

Often the choices were not ours to make. Ultimately, property owners would decide the uses we put their buildings to. Some grew to trust in our ability to make those decisions, but as the number of property owners grew, so too did the different agendas and expectations.

Some only wanted projects that were likely convert to commercial tenancies. Others wanted the opposite, and took the view that free space should be philanthropic and only go to the most worthy. Some were very hands-on and took an active interest in the lives and careers of their tenants while others probably couldn't have told you who they were.

Our agenda was a commitment to the experiment—to a diversity of simultaneous experiments. The goal was not to ensure that everything appealed to everyone but to hope that in that diversity, everyone could find at least something that appealed. Over time, we would discover and collect up viable niches. The city would gradually evolve a collection of things that made sense. It became an eclectic alternative to a suburban shopping centre, and not a pale imitation of it.

We were not afraid of change, but rather needed its own narrative to shift. We changed who got to *own* change, reshaped it from something that was imposed from on high to something that bubbled up from below. We never claimed to know what tomorrow's successful business models were going to look like—we never had a monopoly on what the city was going to be. We knew only that we needed to try things because the city of the future was unknown. We could only discover it by creating it.

Chapter Fifteen—

THE NEW GILDER'S AGE

Ralph Snowball was an enthusiastic and potentially obsessive photographer who died in 1925. He left behind more than 8000 glass negatives of life in Newcastle at the turn of the 20th Century. Many would later be restored, digitised, and shared on Flickr by the University of Newcastle. I learned as much about Newcastle by losing myself in that archive as I had through any study or expert analysis.

One image of Hunter Street at the turn of the 20th Century depicts a 'Manufacturing Jeweller' by the name of Gilder in an elegant bay-windowed shopfront. Outside, a lady is peering intently at the objects in the window.

Another of Snowball's images shows the inside of what may well have been the same shop. In it, there are seven men. They are all dressed in suits, some in white aprons leaning over wooden benches. Others are operating large metal machines. Some are perfectly still—obsessing over fine detail in studied concentration. Their colleagues, meanwhile, are blurred in motion—hammering and drilling too fast for the long exposure and the analogue machine to keep up with.

Today in what may well be the same block—perhaps even the same shop—another group of jewellers occupies a bay-windowed shopfront. Viewers can be found staring at the objects in the window, and inside artisans are engaged in studied concentration or hammering metal into exquisite objects. Studio Melt is a former Renew Newcastle project that began in 2012 and graduated to a full commercial tenancy in only a few months.

It's a studio, teaching space, and sales outlet for local jewellers Angela Hailey and Susie Manning. It was featured in the *Sydney Morning Herald* as an example of a new kind of business model that is supporting regional artisans and craftspeople to get their work to market. It now features, in addition to the work of its owners, about thirty designers whose work ranges from pottery to artwork and textiles.

Studio Melt's ambition is to work with and represent people on a similar scale to its owners—they try to stock items that are unique where possible. They source them both locally and from across Australia. "I want customers to come to us and see things they have never seen before," Angela told the *Sydney Morning Herald*. "I think people walk out feeling very good about having supported someone they had a conversation with."

On one level, the work that Studio Melt does on site is almost a perfect echo of the work once performed by the artisans at Gilders. In another respect though, it is doing something very different. Its makers depend on online stores and networks for much of their business, and on social media such as Instagram and Facebook rather than a captive local audience to drive interest.

Shops like Studio Melt, to me, are the physical manifestation of that invisible but rapidly growing online network of artisans, makers, and jewellers. Its owners run classes to train them. It connects and promotes them. If you walk in there, Susie and Angela can probably tell you not just where everything came from, but the story of the person who made it, and when they last spoke to them.

For lack of a better word, I have come to refer to this phenomenon as 'peertailing'. While Renew participants are required to make what they do, most of the retail businesses quickly evolve towards this kind of peer-based model as they move out on their own.

There is a growing movement of these reciprocal curated networks of makers, curators and artisans. It stretches well beyond Newcastle to cities and towns around the world, where people are opening stores that not only stock and sell their own wares, but pride themselves on seeking out a distinctive selection of others'.

While it is a long way from the days when Gilders made and sold its work onsite, in some ways it is far closer to that than it is to the retail that I grew up with. It is a world away from the idea that a factory in China churns out 100,000 identical units to be stocked in two hundred stores with identical branding, fit-outs and stock placement to be sold by a teenager on minimum wage.

Instead, hundreds of stores around the country and around the world are each curating a distinctive and unique selection of handmade, bespoke, and small volume products. Each and every store is staffed by someone with a unique collection and a unique connection to the work and the person who made it.

A block along from Studio Melt, there is another business with a similar story. It is one with a very different demographic, but it is another manifestation of the same phenomenon. Nook Store too began as a Renew Newcastle project. Nook, which took its name from the pokey, awkward corner space it originally occupied, is a collaboration between three local design labels.

It makes t-shirts, skateboards and streetwear. Its mission is to 'showcase the passionate, independent brands that are emerging within Newcastle' and, like Studio Melt, it does so both in person and online. When Nook's originators first came to us they were barely out of their teens, but they too have grown up and gone commercial.

Nook has built a business that promotes its own labels locally and nationally. In-store, it mixes them with complementary products and like-minded independent labels from around Australia. As the local online magazine HUNTERhunter noted, the experience of niche stores like Nook is quite different to the retailers that had come before them.

'Gone are the days,' HUNTERhunter wrote, 'where blokes awkwardly wander through big old fashioned department stores, sifting through rack after rack, or getting their girlfriends to do it, hoping to find something a little less mainstream.'

While there are no surviving Ralph Snowball images of skaters and streetwear labels, there is a clear connection to a tradition when tailors once made and sold clothes for men here and the factory up the road made bicycles.

In another shop a block along from Nook, Shannon Hartigan

is a self-taught and multi-award-winning landscape photographer. To the extent that Renew Newcastle taught him anything, it was almost certainly not to rely on passing trade. His evolution into a full-fledged photography business began life in a less-than desirable '80s era arcade.

It had once been a thoroughfare between a bridge to the harbour that is no longer there, and a council car park which these days is perpetually under-utilised. Suffice to say there was little foot traffic, and few if any casual photography buyers.

In person Shannon is modest, reserved, and reticent to talk up his own work. But you wouldn't guess that from the adept way he uses Facebook to tell the stories behind his photoshoots, to document his travels, to show off his images and to promote his commissions for high-profile clients. When I first wrote about him, I watched in a browser window as one of his images—a striking panorama of Newcastle—was picked up by a prominent tourism page and quickly went viral, with 30,000 Facebook likes and counting.

His tenacity and talent have taken his imagery to audiences well beyond the dead-end arcade. They have allowed him to grow his business from a fledgling experiment in a once-empty shop to a building he now owns in a far better location around the corner.

The Renew Newcastle projects that have thrived aren't for the most part connected by demographics or styles. Niches like jewellery, skateboards, and landscape photography don't particularly overlap. Their common ground can be found in their distribution chains, their marketing platforms and their business models.

Their approach is very different from the previous wave of

retailers that had foundered here. They don't simply sell things to passers-by. They have grown out of or grown into larger networks that send their wares to outlets and audiences much further afield. I have seen bicycle bells designed and made in Renew studios being sold in bespoke bike stores in Melbourne; coffee cups from Newcastle Productions can be found in cafés in Cooma. I spotted Newcastle-made jewellery in a small store in Wellington, New Zealand.

Where once the retail businesses on this strip would have stood or fallen by the size of the foot traffic and the local market, they now have other paths. Those that are succeeding are doing so across multiple locations and channels—online and physical. The smallest of studio projects are using websites, markets, social media and online stores as secondary and often primary forms of distribution.

The economies of scale of producing one niche product in a mid-sized regional city might once have been a dead end. Now, opportunities online, in stores run by their peers, and in inexpensive physical spaces mean that small manufacturers are building increasingly resilient micro-economies. With low overheads and supportive communities, places like Newcastle suddenly have a competitive advantage. What once would have required a strong local economy is increasingly *stimulating* that economy by bringing money in from outside.

Most of the Renew Newcastle projects that have gone on to have viable business models, sign commercial leases, or even buy their own buildings are ones that would have been marginal if not impossible in the 20th Century. They are working in categories, such as online publishing and digital media, that have only recently been created. They are catalysing communities that would once have been nearly impossible to find. Often, they are using technologies and services that were non-existent or impractically expensive until very recently as their major means of marketing and distribution.

We have learned that this kind of activity can drive the revival of a place. To some extent, there has always been a Catch-22 for unsuccessful shopping strips, precincts, and places. There is no point opening a shop if there are no customers, and often the disinterested tenants themselves become the bane of many failing strip malls and arcades. I've seen dozens of these places. They are half empty, in some cases closed off, literally shuttered up at one end or other. Often they are full of uninviting spaces used for storage and offices rather than retail.

These flailing strips are peppered with tenancies that seem to do everything but activate the place: clubs that meet once a month; an accountant, the only one in the town without a computer, who never seems to be there; a travel agent with fading signs for defunct airlines in the windows. Often mixed in is a single quirky shop—they seem to be the last bastion of vinyl record shops in a lot of towns—that you need to persevere past half a dozen dusty 'Closing Down' signs to find. Collectively they send a powerful signal: 'Turn around, there is nothing to see here!'

Whether it was by accident or by design, Renew Newcastle discovered a sweet spot. People would be present—our agreements actually required it. Their projects would be well-presented, engaging and attractive but would not be dependent on customers who weren't there yet. They didn't rely on the marketing and presence of others to bring them their audience because they brought their own.

Bringing these kind of businesses together began to bring back the foot traffic, to bring in the people that sought them out. It stimulated curiosity and tourism. It created a dynamic around which another wave of businesses, services, bars, cafés and restaurants began to take root.

Retail has always been tough going. It has only become harder recently. We haven't really changed that. In a sense, Newcastle is a microcosm of the uncertainty of changing retail in general. Retail has had to create a new identity. It is not the 'centre of town' anymore. For the most part, Renew has not been a catalyst for bringing back the kind of high street retailers that have fled to the suburbs and moved to the shopping centres. It has been an opportunity to discover something different—a collection of niches. Local products that have national and global audiences. Tourism.

In Newcastle it's still uncertain whether the high rents of the high street, the proposed big shopping centres and some of the more ambitious developments will ever return. But at least the people have.

Chapter Sixteen—

ACTION AND REACTION

In late 2010 I got a phone call. It was from Shawn Low, the Asia Pacific editor at Lonely Planet. The world's largest travel publisher would shortly announce that Newcastle had been included on a list of top travel destinations and their media people suspected the decision would be...I think his word was 'contentious'.

As it would be his job to talk about it, he was planning a visit and wanted some leads and information. The reason he had rang me, he said, was because Renew Newcastle was a main reason for Newcastle's inclusion.

A few weeks later, the publishing house released *Lonely Planet's Best in Travel 2011*. I had assumed, wrongly as it turned out, that the list in question would be a local one. Instead, they had placed Newcastle just a few notches below New York City as one of the top ten cities to visit in the world that year.

'Australia's most underrated city,' they wrote, had

transformed itself 'from 'steel city' to creative hub' with 'an explosion of artists... photographers, fashion designers, digital artists and more as part of the inner-city regeneration scheme Renew Newcastle.'

Confirming Shawn's prediction, the *Newcastle Herald* wrote somewhat understatedly that 'Sydney has never made the list before so to have Newcastle in the top 10 was controversial.' Over the coming months, my Google Alert for 'Renew Newcastle' was suddenly tracking mentions from more than a dozen countries. I was answering constant questions from international travel writers. It was a gimmick, but it was a most welcome one.

It's impossible for me to write objectively about what Renew Newcastle has achieved. It's a story most easily told in pictures: before and after photos. But here, it is probably easiest just to start with the numbers.

Over six years, we have launched more than a hundred and seventy initiatives, community projects and businesses. They have ranged in size from the low-budget partial conversion of an empty department store to short exhibitions and countless one- and two-person artist studios and creative businesses. With our help, the people behind those projects have cleaned up and reopened more than seventy previously vacant properties. Today I can't think of any of them that are empty again.

Newcastle has weathered the downturn in retail and the global headwinds better than most places on earth. The first week I had met with property owners was the same week that Lehman Brothers collapsed. While financial capital dried up, Newcastle had gone into the Global Financial Crisis with a system to martial human capital that no other city had.

Since then the inner city of Newcastle has seen a 60–90% drop in vacancy rates. Surveys by Newcastle NOW, the local business traders association, have shown that while retail vacancies were on the rise in cities around the world, in Newcastle they have been steadily disappearing.

Where the *Newcastle Herald* had once written of a mall of more than twenty empty shops, today there are almost none. I have scores of photos of boarded-up buildings and 'For Lease' signs where today there are new shops, new restaurants, new bars, cafés and a growing cluster of mostly local, mostly independent businesses. More than twenty of Renew Newcastle's projects have grown and graduated into full rent-paying commercial businesses.

Like all small businesses, some of those have survived and thrived while others have fallen by the wayside. Around them there are many others that can trace at least part of their lineage back to people, events and activities that had been catalysed by Renew. Others have simply moved in on the rising tide of activity, confidence and foot traffic that has come through the city.

Despite decades of big plans, Newcastle is still a city in transition. Parts of it are still in limbo. GPT's proposed development was a casualty of the financial crisis. David Sleet, who had championed the project, was for a time a casualty too. He was briefly laid off by the company before, I'm pleased to say, being reemployed on another project. Now GPT is a minor partner. It has sold the controlling stake in the site to Urban Growth, a government development agency that continues to actively support Renew Newcastle.

Over the years the program has grown to involve more than a dozen property owners from multinational companies to Mum-and-Dad investors. Today there are more than sixty projects and nearly thirty properties that are running under the umbrella of Renew Newcastle. They spread from Newcastle East to Newcastle West.

In 2012, an independent review of the Renew model conducted by SGS Economics and Planning found that there was a range of quantifiable benefits to the scheme. It found that Renew had reduced blight and anti-social behaviour, improved business and community confidence, developed skills, engaged thousands of hours of volunteer time, created intellectual capital and jobs, reduced maintenance and other costs to property owners, and improved regional brand value, tourism and inward investment. It also found that Renew Newcastle had a 10.8 to 1 benefit cost ratio — every dollar spent on it came back nearly elevenfold in other benefits.

New South Wales tourism data found that tourism to Newcastle had grown by more than half a million extra visitors a year since Renew Newcastle began. It was among the highest growth rates in the state. It had come at a time when tourism in Australia has been struggling. The projects we supported had appeared not just in Lonely Planet, but in dozens of travel features, in-flight magazines and tourism articles across Australia and around the world. In 2014, a local tourism survey found the Hunter Street Mall was the second most popular destination in the city behind only the iconic Nobby's Beach.

Along the way there have been countless accolades and awards. We have won local, state, and national economic development awards. Despite not living in Newcastle I was made 'Citizen of the Year' in 2010. Shortly afterwards, GPT and

Renew Newcastle won the Australia Business Arts Foundation National Partnership of the Year Award—the highest award in Australia for arts philanthropy. It was up against a who's who of Australia's largest companies, individuals and the most well resourced arts organisations.

When Marni Jackson moved on from Renew and from Newcastle after five years, her decision to leave was met with the kind of local media coverage usually reserved for a retiring sports star. She had earned it.

Very quickly, the story and the model had percolated in other contexts. Versions of it—some significantly embellished or mistranslated—had been told well outside my comfort zone of Australian art and media. Returning to Newcastle I had thought I was choosing—or at least being sucked into—a labour of love that would be of little interest to anyone outside. Renew Newcastle has proved to be a universal story, and not just a local one.

It is a model that has brought interest from people, professions, and places not just across Australia but around the world. I have spoken to audiences about Renew in Amsterdam, Cardiff, Christchurch, Copenhagen, Denver, London, New York, Santiago, Sheffield, Toronto, and scores of major cities and country towns across Australia.

It has resonated with the architects and urban planners. Rory Hyde, the author, architect, writer, and curator of Contemporary Architecture and Urbanism at London's V&A Museum, has written of Renew Newcastle as 'an incredibly important model for the regeneration of urban areas ... through its unique combination of people, spaces, and encouraging of creative entrepreneurialism.'

The British writer, designer and urbanist Dan Hill described it as 'one of the most innovative and interesting urban projects to have emerged anywhere in the last decade or so—I use it constantly as a shining example of how to make cities work.'

It has found interest too from economists and economic writers. Justin Fox , *Time* magazine's then economics editor, was convinced by my argument 'that commercial real estate is prone to market failure.' The case was 'pretty striking' and Renew's 'clever partial solution' to the 'the cost of complying with regulation can make small businesses and small real estate transactions uneconomic' was lauded.

Felix Salmon, writing for Reuters, took a similar view, writing, 'commercial real estate in general often stays empty for extremely long periods of time—something which harms neighborhoods and lets huge amounts of economic value go to waste. Occasionally someone like Marcus Westbury will come along and shake things up.'

Those interested in technology and democracy also took an interest. The website TechPresident described Renew Newcastle as having 'hacked the real estate industry'—giving me a metaphor I have used ever since. Bruce Sterling wrote about the model in his blog at *Wired* with the gently understated observation that 'There is genius in this.'

In Australia perhaps the most striking aspect has been the way in which the reception to the project defied the political boxes and simple left/right characterisation. Renew Newcastle and the model behind it has been praised across the political spectrum. It has been embraced by conservative rural mayors and inner-city activists.

I have spoken at events organised by property developers and business chambers, and by Liberal and Labor Party politicians. I've driven across the wilds of Tasmania with the federal leader of the Green Party and lunched in the north of the state with a campaign manager for its conservative opponents. Renew has been held up as a pro-business scheme and as a model of arts, community involvement and participation.

Given that slightly bewildering paradox, it is inevitable that Renew Newcastle has been the subject of critical investigation and academic interest. Much of it has attempted to probe and unpack the same contradictions that allow it to be lauded on both left and right. Is it neoliberalism, or an alternative to it? Does it invite and encourage gentrification? Is it a potential catalyst for displacement? Who will benefit and who will miss out? Those are all questions that occupy me too, although the jury is still out on the answers.

For now the academic questions speak less to the specific context of Newcastle and more about cautionary tales from other places. They raise lessons from New York, London, Berlin, San Francisco, Sydney, and Melbourne about the dangers and challenges of successes not yet not entirely realised.

Back in Newcastle the critics are more prosaic. On the street, the most common worry is that some people are getting a free ride. Some assume, incorrectly, that the city is full of shops on taxpayer subsidies and large arts grants and not merely borrowed space. There is a scepticism that these shops selling 'junk' and 'knick knacks' aren't real businesses, or that the jobs created aren't real jobs. That Renew is a diversion and a distraction from the real work that still needs to take place.

A significant section of the community is still impatient for the big change and the delivery of big promises. They view

Renew not as iterative process, but as stop-gap that will end when real change arrives—the 'proper' developments that are still just over the horizon. Some think Renew has succeeded and served its purpose, while others have seen nothing change and nothing to take credit for.

Perhaps the greatest success and challenge for Renew Newcastle is that it has created a new normal. The state of the city a decade ago has receded into distant memory. What is there now was always going to be there. People now have the luxury of comparing it not to the broken and dysfunctional place from which this journey began, but to the mythologised past where everything just *worked.*

Others look to the future and compare it to an imperfect present. Against the artists' illustrations, the ambitions, the plans and the promises, what has actually happened is still a disappointment.

From where I sit, the long-term impact is probably just too soon to tell. What will ultimately emerge from the tensions between development and decay, germination and gentrification, commerce and community can only be resolved and revealed by the passage of time.

I do believe that we have changed the city for the better. That the actions of hundreds of people have created a new dynamic, and that that dynamic will live on and feed into whatever may happen next. I am sure that we have created things that will live on long after Renew Newcastle disappears and, for the foreseeable future, we will continue creating things. Whether that is a net win or a loss will be debated and discussed, analysed and interpreted and measured against what happens in Newcastle and elsewhere. It will be for others to judge.

Perhaps the most important changes are invisible and intangible. They are in imagination and expectations. Edwina Richards, of Make Space, sent me a story about the influence it had had on her children:

> My ten-year-old boy had to write an article for his school newspaper about 'A Newcastle Icon.' He chose Renew Newcastle. He was proud. He had a personal story to tell, and he was inspired to tell it. He was just five years old when he helped pull up the carpet in the first Make Space shop and rode his skateboard through an empty silent Mall when he got sick of painting walls.
>
> My kids now see empty shops and they imagine what they might become. A disco, a joke shop, a café where they serve only cream pies and throw them at you. They see the city of their childhood as a playground. They see adults playing with ideas and materials and working together to make things happen with very little resources. I've personally had a blast. I've made lifelong friends, I feel like I'm part of a creative community, and learned so much. But that impression on my children is my proudest achievement.

If Renew Newcastle is nothing more than a sign on a hill I will happily take it.

Part Five—

ON REFLECTION

Chapter Seventeen—

THE VIEW FROM THE EDGE

I have a slideshow now. It changes depending on the audience and to keep myself interested, but it often follows the same basic form. It begins with the 'before' slides: the decay, the abandoned and empty buildings. These are the photos Narinda and I took during that long walk looking for a bar space and on those early trips back and forth, of boarded up-windows, derelict and burnt-out buildings, and lonely figures in front of 'For Lease' signs on otherwise empty streets.

As I tell the story the slides gradually change. The decay begins to give way to little interventions, to people with brushes and brooms, and modest jury-rigged fit-outs. Some audiences will make the odd audible "wow" at some of the low budget make-overs. I tell anecdotes of individual achievement and unlikely successes. Some stories I've told so many times I've forgotten where they came from. I'm not even sure if they're true anymore.

If I've ordered it chronologically, you can literally see the streets evolve. More and more better-presented places. More and more people around. Towards the end there is a usually a map—it is never up to date because things still change too quickly. It shows a before-and-after, with some hundred-and-fifty red dots where the empty buildings were. It dissolves and reveals the scores of green-dotted sites where Renew Newcastle is and has been, and shows how many of the red dots have disappeared.

Once I was showing these pictures and telling this story in Sydney, to an audience from local government, business, and the arts. At the end a senior policy maker at the City of Sydney got up to ask the first question. "That's great," she said, "but what if you don't have all the advantages of Newcastle?"

There is a cliché that artists inevitably gravitate towards and transform run-down areas. It has become so ingrained in our thinking that we've forgotten that for most places, it isn't actually true. In big cities like Sydney and Melbourne, it has been happening in concentric circles, radiating out from the centre of the city. It has happened in Berlin and in Brooklyn.

In these tales of gentrification, it is easy to debate cause and effect. To what extent artists are to be blamed or credited is up in the air, but the results are clear enough. Poor communities near the centres of rich major cities are often on the wrong end of gentrification. Cheap space in and around the centre of the world's wealthy cities is becoming a thing of the past.

Travel through declining Australian regional towns, to rust-belt cities across the US, to main streets and strip malls in outer suburban communities, or to towns in Europe that have lost their industries and are struggling to keep their young people.

These are places stalled or stranded by the financial crisis. There are no hordes of hipsters to magically transform them. Away from the tourist strips and the centres of finance, most of the world is a lot more like Newcastle than New York.

The reality is not that failing towns inevitably attract the attention of innovators, artists, cool kids, or entrepreneurs who displace their communities and destroy their character. The reality is that they mostly don't. Mostly, they splutter. Sometimes, they fail. Often, like Newcastle, they wait in limbo for the big fix. They become vulnerable to illusionary quick fixes and con men.

If they are lucky they are reinvented and revitalised by governments or sympathetic developers who knock things down and build apartments, or factories, or shopping malls. If they're unlucky, they slowly die.

It is easy to misunderstand what Renew has done and is trying to achieve: 'Hip artists take over industrial town—you won't believe what happened next!' In reality it is not and *never has been* an exercise in attracting the 'creative class'. It is not a marketing exercise to rebrand Newcastle as a 'creative city'. It is certainly not a billion-dollar attempt at being the new Bilbao.

It is not an attempt to lure big brands and become a trendy hotbed of corporate creativity, and it is not about iconic buildings or star architects. It is not about the veneer of vibrancy. The lessons from Renew Newcastle are not about how to transform your community into a global centre of the creative industries. They are about what to do when you can't.

I never thought I would see a day when anyone in Sydney would be even remotely concerned about "all the advantages of Newcastle" but as it transpires, at least some of Newcastle's problems were indeed its opportunities. Newcastle was broken but in many respects it was an ideal place to start. Its architecture and natural landscape were an asset. It was an old and established city—at least by Australian standards. It had a variety of styles and shapes and scales of spaces.

Waves of economic development had largely passed it by, leaving the character of many of its older buildings intact. It is still a place with a rich mix of building stock, and not simply a failed property play that had been rolled out overnight. It had changed, adapted and evolved many times, to accommodate many uses over many years. But its biggest advantage was that it already had much of what it needed—the dots just hadn't been connected yet.

Renew is a case study about the value of looking inward. Newcastle has changed not by attracting new and cool people to it, but largely from bringing out the talents and the capabilities of the people who were already there. In that sense, it is not unique. As I began to travel, to show those slides and tell this story, I was surprised by the kinds of people I met in towns and suburbs. I'm not anymore.

In most towns, there's usually someone who will attempt to explain that this wouldn't work there, because they don't have creative people who are doing or making anything that would fit with this kind of model. A minute later someone will put their hand up and tell a story that contradicts the claim. Then another, and another. So far there is nowhere I've been where the number of people with ideas they wanted to try didn't outnumber the number of spaces that were desperate to be used.

For most communities, the idea that creative people might seek to act on their imagination and invest it in improving the life, economic and employment prospects, or even just the visual amenity of the place is a good thing. There is little downside. In a failing suburb, a town, or a small city with difficult challenges, such creative approaches are, at the very least, a good first option. They are the least disruptive and the most realistic.

Compared to the capital-intensive and expensive approaches that many places are holding out for, approaches like Renew involve little risk, low up-front costs, and the highest probability of at least a few quick wins and modest successes.

For places that aren't at the centre—that aren't Brooklyn or Soho or San Fran—the pendulum has gradually begun to swing in their favour. Technology has changed what is possible, so that the demographic and economic advantages of living in a major city have become less and less important for some particular kinds of things. The prerequisites for creative and community initiatives are becoming far more widespread and democratised than they have been at any point in human history.

Down here Down Under, rapid changes in the circulation of ideas are particularly noticeable. For a long time, our culture and economy has been defined by our isolation. Little more than a generation ago, information was slow to arrive. It took the knowledge of migrants or travellers, and long-delayed (and overpriced) media and other physical connection points to the wider world for us to know what was happening. It took a ship or a plane to bring the ideas and inspiration from the wider world *here*.

Whether we liked it or not, our culture was relatively insular, and isolated by its lack of connectivity with the wider world. We needed people who travelled widely or read exhaustively to bring in new ideas or possibilities. The regional Australia of my childhood was full of (potentially apocryphal) stories of how the local restaurant owner had 'discovered' the idea of *al fresco* dining on a trip to Spain, or of how a new café had been inspired by someone's first trip to Melbourne.

Today, everything is *here*. For better or for worse, our communities are being substantially changed by technology. The downside is obvious in every empty bookstore; the upside is that things are changing the trajectories and possibilities of local places, and the ways in which ideas and inspiration are circulating in the world. Since I began working on this project there have been recurring reminders of how ideas, memes and inspiration can spread at an instant from one side of the world to another.

Renew Newcastle is part of a global dialogue with place-makers, tactical urbanists, pop-up practitioners, guerrilla gardeners, architects, better blockers and urban interventionists. We can see so much of the world now, not just its highlights. We can see its details, its problems, and so many of its ingenious little solutions. There are things to learn and lessons to teach. I have stolen other people's best ideas and encouraged them to steal mine.

That same connectivity is echoed too through each and every project. Each is a microcosm of a wider network. Each is distinctive. Most of them are very much from and of Newcastle; they literally could not have happened anywhere else. Yet virtually all of them are connected. They are part of global movements, networks, dialogues and markets.

We have all been given the capacity to view the places we live in through the eyes of the migrant or the well-worn traveller.

We can see it for what it is and what it is not. We can look at our places, compare them to others, and ask *why not*? All of us now have a frame through which we might see and seek, and more importantly, to *act* in our own communities.

It is that last piece that is the most important. People *want* to participate. They don't just want to be asked what professionals should do on their behalf. People want to be Bert Webber again, building signs and claiming stakes in their communities. Civic leaders need to think of it as their job to work out how to tap into, accommodate, and enable that motivation, and inspire and engage their citizens in action.

Perhaps the most damaging myth of all is the idea that artists or creatives or whatever you want to call them are somehow special. That people who do things are some kind of 'other' force that butts up against the *status quo* with special insights and talents and visions. I don't actually think that's true.

It is the very ordinariness of action and imagination that I find reassuring. It is the diversity of people and places it comes from that I find solace in. It is the realisation that the propensity for imagination and action is a force like any other. It responds to invitations and opportunities, to collaborations and connections, and often lies dormant within communities and individuals.

The most important aspect of technology—particularly social media—is its ability to connect inspiration to organisation. We need to give it things to organise. The city itself is the experiment. The city is the laboratory. This is the test bed. Its buildings are the raw ingredients; its rules and governance structures are its levers and its test tubes. Its citizens are its catalysts.

The challenge is to provide a framework that allows those

experiments to be run. It is certainly not to determine what the outcomes should be. It is not to try to second-guess too much. It is not to limit opportunity to the select few who are rich and resourceful, but to ensure that the possibility of participation is shared as equitably as possible with everyone. It is to softly and gently encourage and curate and enable and activate that desire of citizens to *do*.

Chapter Eighteen—

FAILING TO FAIL ENOUGH

Renew Newcastle is a fudge. In an ideal world—regardless of how your particular ideologically imagines it—such fudges, kludges, brokers, fixers and intermediaries should have no need to exist.

In a perfect capitalist market, the laws of supply and demand would kick in and ensure that every resource is allocated to the most efficient use. There would be no empty buildings. Under utopian socialism, property would be taken from the greedy and given to the needy. In some anarchic alternate universe, wasted space would be occupied by agitators and activists, squatters and scholars, communities and communes with no regard for the petty complexities and bureaucracies that make getting stuff done tricky.

But we don't live in any of those worlds. We live in a world bound up by contradictions and contests of philosophies, of mixed signals and unintended consequences. A world that is complicated and difficult to understand, where the need for things to happen quickly is battered against processes that grind slowly, and at times, not at all.

This is a world that can allocate resources badly, where development dynamics can detach from the actual needs of people in local communities. Where speculation and doing nothing can grow dollar values while potential is squandered and the tangible values of real things, real lives, and real communities are depreciated and destroyed.

It is easy to forget that very few people are experienced at being inexperienced. Being new to a problem is inherently transitional. People who succeed forget their early challenges and move on to bigger ones, and successful projects take on an aura of retrospective inevitability. The serendipities and support structures from which they emerged are forgotten.

Failed things often sink with little trace and nothing learned. Those that never were are rarely even noticed by their absence. The idea that we might be failing to fail enough is deeply counterintuitive.

There are at least two types of failure. The first is the type of error that is intrinsically linked with trial—the process of discovering what works, and what doesn't, by doing it. The second failure is more insidious. It is a cultural failure, a self-perpetuating one whereby the expectation that nothing can succeed becomes so powerful that no one tries anything at all. The first kind of failure is a necessary precondition for success. The second can be terminal.

We need to start building places and environments that initiative is attracted to. We rarely talk about initiative; we don't really have the language for it. It's a category error. We are trained by the disciplines we work in to see initiative as something else. It is common to hear talk of investment, of attracting capital and stimulating entrepreneurialism, or seeding 'community'. But as the experience of Renew developed, I began to realise that what we often mean and need is initiative.

We literally don't value it. We find it hard to measure. The actions that make for better places, the things that make a community more cohesive and connected, the things that cause lives to become meaningful and places to transform don't always translate seamlessly to a spreadsheet. Fortunately, the world is full of people who don't much care.

Small-scale initiative has almost no one to speak for it, because it isn't organised that way. Its practitioners are too busy, stuck in the practicalities of getting stuff done. They are tired, and tied up with their own immediate barriers and concerns. They struggle to separate systemic problems from personal ones. They mostly think that failure is their fault. Even when they know the system is broken, they lack the resources, the influence, the expertise and the time to actually do anything about it.

So how do we help them? It is easy to get it wrong. Systems to support people can often founder on first principles—they become extensions of the bureaucracies from which they have grown. Poorly designed, they become just another layer of complexity. They work on time-scales that sap momentum. It can take months or years to get an idea up, find the right program, and establish eligibility. But enthusiasm can fade, moments get lost, and windows of opportunity can quickly close.

It is hard to pick winners. The sheer diversity of possibilities and ideas make it problematic, if not impossible. The splintering of audiences and markets makes it politically and practically difficult. Between art, entrepreneurialism, digital cottage industries, a movement of makers, and potentially profitable enterprise, the question of what communities should invest in is problematic.

Do you invest in what has the greatest potential, or the greatest need? Do you invest where there is a market, or where there is market failure? Do you take a leap on untested ideas, or follow trends? There is no easy right or wrong answer to these questions. There are cases for all of them, and cases for none.

I keep coming back to the question of risk, to ideas not of what do we need to succeed but of how things might fail here. In some places that thinking has started to permeate. There are public and private 'incubators,' 'hubs' and 'start-up zones,' but these are often preoccupied with outcomes that are high-tech and highly profitable.

Most of the creative and community risk that I am interested in is low-tech, marginally profitable (in a narrow financial sense), unglamorous and mundane. 90% of tech start-ups fail. You can invest in the idea of the 10–1 long shot if the payoff is a hundredfold. The logic unravels when the risks and the returns are small.

Renew Newcastle is an exercise in creating fertile ground. It is imperfect, carved out of compromises and contexts over which it has little or no control. Nonetheless, it has done enough to demonstrate that there is value in that ambition, and to show what fertile ground can yield.

Not everywhere needs a Renew Newcastle. Each place has its own problems and potential. Some places already do many of these things better than we do, and some have challenges of geography, poverty, ideology and opportunity that a Renew Newcastle alone will do little to correct.

But every community *should* aspire to fertile ground. It should be someone's job not just to dream of and plan for ambitious outcomes, but to work, doggedly and systematically, through the small things. To slog through the process of doing, and get down into the layers of mundane challenges. To make sure the actual process of acting on an idea works for the people who are trying to do it.

Fertile ground requires thinking about and taking ownership of the gaps in existing processes. Government, business and the community all have a role to play in bringing each part of the process a little closer to the one before it, ensuring that each rung on the ladder can be reached from the rung below.

Physical communities can learn real lessons from why and how communities of creativity have flourished online. People will climb higher and faster if the rungs are within reach, and if it is safe enough to fall or slip a rung or two and know the consequences won't be fatal.

Lowering barriers, as opposed to picking winners, should not require a political, financial or practical consensus around doing any individual thing. It still leaves it to the market or the community in its willingness to support an idea to determine whether any given project survives, thrives or dies.

What it *does* require is a conscious decision to make small things easy. To promote and encourage them; to give them places to start, paths to grow and develop. To allow our cities to be platforms for ideas that might not work in order to discover ideas that do.

Ultimately, the most import thing for communities to do

is to find ways to lower the price and risk of participation. We need to remove the binary and often arbitrary distinction between the amateur and the professional and turn it into a smooth continuum. We need to extend an invitation to everyone in the community to act and meet their needs in whichever ways we can.

We need systems that are proportional to the risk and rewards of what people want to do. We need to recognise that most people have things to invest that aren't capital, and that some seek rewards and returns that aren't always about money.

There are lessons for most places in what has happened in Newcastle. Every community—not merely ones that are in despair or decay—needs to encourage experimentation. The specific answers to the problems, the specific enablers, and the local solutions will be as diverse as the communities themselves.

Cities and places spend a lot of time on attracting commercial investment and chasing government grants. They think a lot about how to entice bankers and builders, developers and dollars, investors and entrepreneurs. Hardly ever do they ask themselves how they might get people to invest their initiative there.

How to encourage old men to take responsibility for the signage problems of their ailing parklands. How to get kids to clean out and open up empty buildings. How to get suburban mums and dads to open a shop or plant a community garden.

Communities where *all* citizens can act on their desire to create, to build, to organise, experiment and create are healthy, resilient, and constructive ones. A healthy society is one where the contest of ideas can play out by example, and not by one group denying others the opportunity to participate. Communities need people to be able to act on their imaginations. People need to be able shape the communities that they live in by what they do and not just by what they spend.

I suspect that the reason that Renew is so bewildering to people who want to position it on the left-right spectrum is that this isn't the spectrum it acts upon. Renew operates on the axis of big and small. Both governments and markets, left and right can be equally guilty of privileging the macro over the micro.

Renew is, more than anything else, a strategy for the *small.* It is a business incubator *and* it's a community scheme. It's an arts initiative *and* it's an economic development one. It is a strategy for young *and* for old. It works because it is at that smallest moment—the one where someone might pick up a paintbrush, a shovel, put on a show or set up a store—that there is the most immediate capacity for action. It reduces at least some problems down to a size at which people can actually fix them.

It is at the small scale where you will find the most squandered opportunities for rapid transformation. Where there is resilience, diversity and opportunity. Great places come from organic experiments. They come from accumulated trial and error that takes place over years and decades. They are discovered as much as they are just planned. It is the initiative of people that is the raw material from which interesting and successful places are made. It is the connection of people from which cohesion and social capital are developed.

It is from the smallest of scales that grand possibilities can be built up.

ACKNOWLEDGEMENTS

I personally would not be here without the support of my family: Narinda in all her unyielding awesomeness and our two boys Louin and Otto. Words can't do justice to how much I love you guys. I'd also like the thank Narinda's mum Thess and my brother Stuart for all their support over the years and the extended Hannah family for repeatedly lending me a place to hide and to write.

Renew Newcastle and Renew Australia have benefited from the support of too many people to mention. None of this would be possible without the support of our team, the board members, property owners and all the people that have shared, engaged with and supported our work. Some of them are named in this book. Many of them are not simply because any such list would inevitably be impossible and incomplete.

Renew in its various guises has now helped launch more than two hundred projects in towns and cities across Australia and a few more around the world. The passion and efforts of all those people and the ability to be a small part of what they achieve is something I take great pride in. Thank you to all of them.

In many ways the making of this book is an extension of the same ideas, possibilities and culture that seeded Renew in the first place. For *Creating Cities* to become a book has taken the efforts of many people. Like everything I've ever done it's a collaboration. I'd like to single out my editor Jessica Friedmann for her support and assistance in carving a book out from the mess of notes and brain dumps that this originally began with.

Our small production team of Sarah Bunting, Marnie Kay, Damien Frost and Michael Carolan are also greatly appreciated. I would also like to thank Jim Kellar, Chad Watson, Lisa Anderson, Edwina Richards, Phil Ashley-Brown and Lisa Pryor for prompt assistance with clearing rights to use material I have quoted. I'd particularly thank Julianne Schultz at *Griffith REVIEW* whose invitation to write a piece about cities and culture inadvertently set off this chain of events.

Most importantly, this book is a result of a crowd funding campaign that was contributed to by more than 900 people. My thanks to Stu McBratney for putting the video together and the team at Pozible for their support at several key points. The support (and patience) of every single person who has contributed has been crucial in making this happen and I hope that they are happy with the finished product – despite the fact it took a little longer than promised!

My particular thanks to Ace Wagstaff, Adam Bandt, Adam Hogan, Adeline Teoh, Adrian Dale, Adrienne Dite, Alan Crabbe, Alex J Taylor, Alex Kelly, Alicia Darvall, Alysha Herrmann, Alysia Bennett, Amadeo Marquez-Perez, Amanda Benson, Amanda Kunkler, Amie Grierson, Andrew E Dickinson, Andrew Lewis, Andrew Spannenberg, Andrew Wisdom, Ann Caddey, Ann Hardy, Anna Gerber, Anna Kinsky Walker, Anna Yeates, Anthony Aisenberg, Ashleigh Ryan, Atticus & Jack Bristow, Barbara Schaffer Bacon, Bec Hawkings, Becky Elwing, Ben May, Ben Milbourne, Benjamin Greaves, Benjamin Law, Bernadette Wilson, Beth Nelson, BKK Architects, Blueberry Paper, Bob Shaw, Brendan Brooks,

Brent Smith, Brenton Caffin, Brian Hill, Brigid Noone, Brooke Small, Bruce Esplin, Burger Theory, Caitlin Vaughan, Camilla Tierney, Camille Short, Carla Bergen, Carole Rigler, Caroline Le Couteur, Carolyn Stewart, Cat Turner, Cate Turner, Catherine Hart, Catherine Stanton, Catina Adams, Centre for Creative Arts (Latrobe University), Chantel Carr, Cheryl McMaster, Chloe Beevers, Chris Grist, Chris Miller, Chris Muir, Chris Newton, Chris Winter, Chris Womersley, Christopher Saunders, Cindi Drennan, Cindy Plowman, Claire Mooney, Cobi Smith, Colin Fairweather, Constance Mehel, Coralie Winn, Corinne Paterson, Councillor Rosmairi Dawson, Craig Allchin, Curve Gallery, Damian Callinan, Dan Hinks, Dan Thompson, Daniel Greer, Dave Sag, Dave Sharp, David Barnard, David Cianci, David Hood, David Schloeffel, David Shaw, David Sleet, David Winterton, Dean Cracknell, Debbi Long, Deborah Kelly, Debra Patterson, Deidre But-Husaim, Diana Jones, Digby Hannah, Dominic Knight, Donald Bates, Doug Lithgow, Edmund Carter, Elanor Rooney, Eliza Muldoon, Elizabeth McDonald, Elizabeth Taylor, Ella Barclay, Ella Hinkley, Elliott Bledsoe, Emily Berwyn, Emily Craven, Esther Anatolitis, Esther Sugihto, Evan Baverstock, Ewan McEoin, (f)route, Feargus Manning, Fiona Beckwith, Francesca Ford, Gabi Mika Mcnaughton, Gareth Colliton, Gavin Artz, Geoff ILearn, Gionni Di Gravio, Graham Wilson, Hayden Williams, Hella Bella Bark, Henry Boston,Hub Adelaide, Hub Melbourne, Hub Sydney, Hugh Rundle, Ianto Ware, Icelab, Ingrid Burkett, Ingrid Lees, Jacinta Hayter, Jacqueline Power, Jade Lillie, James Arvanitakis, James Morris, James Riggall, James Vidler, Jan van Schaik, Jane Shadbolt, Janelle McIntosh, Jason Bourke,Jason Elsley, Jason Ridgway,

Jean Poole, Jennifer Greer Holmes, Jeremy Balius, Jeremy Yuille, Jess Scully, Jesse Reynolds, Jo Dyer, Joanne Jakovich, Joanne McNeill, Joe Larkings, John Bardoel, John Irving, John Montgomery, Jonathon Kirkby, Joni Taylor, Jude Anderson, Judith Ridge, Juilee Pryor, Julia Herne, Julie Vulcan, Justine Gaudry, Kat Black, Kat Chish, Kat Muscat, Kate Ryan, Kath ODonnell, Kathryn Gray, Katie Lenanton, Katie O'Rourke, Katie Stubley, Kay Jamieson, Kelly Robson, Kenny Sabir, Kenny Wah Newitt, Kevin O'Brien, Kirsten Bradley, Kris Leck, Kristin Alford, Kristy See, Ksenia Totoeva, Lachlan Musicman, Lachlan William Graham Maslen, Lara Torr, Larry Galbraith, Laura Jean McKay, Laura Wilson, Lee Tran Lam, Lee-Ann Joy, Lena Nahlous, Liga Bennetts, Little Green Corner, Lou Smith, Louisa Connors, Luis Puig, Luke Smith, Luke Snarl Dearnley, Lynne Hughes, Magdalena Moreno, Margaret Spencer, Mariam Arcilla, Mark B Preece, Mark Davis, Mark Fallu, Mark Gill, Mark Jacques, Mark Kennedy, Mark Scott, Mark Seebeck, Mark Wakely, Marni Jackson, Martin Matthews, Martin Quirke, Martin Wilson, Mary Lou Jelbart, Matt Levinson, Matthew Crozier, Matthew Gingold, Matthew Kneale, Matthew Willcox, Mayor Brad Pettitt, Melissa Brendish, Melissa Castan, Melissa Kaulfuss, Melissa So, Melonie Bayl-Smith, Michael Bishop, Michael Spartalis, Michelle van Gestel, Millie Millgate, Miranda Earle, Miriam Lyons, Mitra Rose Anderson-Oliver, MUSK Architecture Studio, Nairn Johnston, Natalie Davey, Natasha Frisch, Nathan Harrison, Neil Mcinroy, Nicholas Carr, Nicholas Pickard, Nicholas Wood, Nick Bastow, Nina Howard, Noel Payne, Owen Tilbury, Owen Williams, Pamela Caspani, Pat Allan, Patrick Pittman, Paul Callaghan, Penelope Benton, Peter Ho, Philip Pollard, pvi collective, Rachael Gill, Rachel

Healy, Rebecca Cunningham, Rebecca Eggleston, Rebecca Grasso, Regional Development Australia Hunter, Richard Cox, Richard Fox, Richard Kervin, Richard Watts, Rita Liao, Rita Siow, Rob Lang, Robert Heather, Rosalea Monacellla, Ross Kerridge, Ross Turnbull, Ruth Bain, Sally Brand, Sally Rosevear, Sam Granleese, Sandra Walsh, Sarah Heald, Sarah McRitchie, Scott Drummond, Seb Chan, Shannon Hartigan, Shannon O'Neill, Sharon Holliday, Shaun Ewing, Sher Campbell, Simeon King, Simeon Moran, Simon Porter, Simon van Praag, Simon Wollan, Simone Sheridan, Siobhan Curran, Stephanie Hinds, Stephen Kerry, Steve Bentley, Steven Alward, Steven Turner, Stuart Buchanan, Stuart Westbury, Susan Kukucka, Suzie Bailey, Tanya Fogarty, Terry Flew, Tess Cox, Thessalie Reeders, Thomas Rivard, Tiffaney Bishop, Tim Brady, Tim Denshire-Key, Tim Roberts, Tim Webster, Timothy Horton, Tony Farrell, Tony Keogh, Trent Middleton, Vanessa Keenan, Vanessa Toulmin, Vivienne Skinner, Walking Melbourne Tours, Wayde Christie, Wendy Carlisle, Wendy Lasica, Wendy Molly Peacock, Zac and Zina Kaye.

My general thanks to everyone who contributed, shared a link, supported the project or supported me along the way.

FLUID CITIES CREATE

What makes a city culturally dynamic? What makes a city the sort of place that people want to visit, move to and explore? What makes a city the sort of place that spits out or draws in artists, musicians, writers and filmmakers? What makes a city culturally desirable and talked about, or a hub of music, literature, media and the arts?

The cultures of cities are far less predictable than their hard infrastructure. You can quantify good transport links, and you can commission public buildings or even the quasi-scientific art of designing successful communities, yet there are few road-maps to apply to the hard task of fostering a dynamic successful culture. It is much more than placement of monuments, buildings or transport links.

Cultures aren't fixed or fixable. They are barely measurable. While you can identify the preconditions that led to Renaissance Italy, early twentieth century Paris, the San

Francisco techno-hippie culture, Hong Kong cinema, the Seattle grunge explosion, Melbourne laneways, the music scenes of Manchester and now Glasgow, or the anarchic wonder of early 'noughties' Berlin, it will never be possible to replicate them.

They are a product of living things and become living things themselves. They're fluids, not solids. Cultures flow. Cultures surge. Cultures stagnate, inundate and flood. Cultures pool and freeze, and in doing so they create another landscape in cities, countries and continents as tangible as the legacy water leaves on smooth plains and jagged mountains on the ever-changing earth. The very act of quantifying these preconditions risks undermining the vitality that produced them.

They aren't transferable. Culture is the process by which we communicate with each other, exchange ideas, explore possibilities, and collect and curate our personal and collective histories. They are the means by which we learn something of each other's lives and experiences, and reflect, respond to and reject inner and outer worlds.

For cities, though, culture takes on another role. Culture is an aspiration. It is a driver of status, and status is bound to wealth and prestige. Global cities increasingly aspire to cultural prestige for its intangible aura and because they believe it will drive economic growth. Wealthy cities race each other to build grander museums and hoard ever more of the world's treasures; poorer cities look to cultural renewal for salvation and rejuvenation.

There is no easy way to buy or build a culture. Culture has properties that defy planning. The more you grab at it, freeze it and attempt to set it in its place, the weaker it becomes. Grand buildings, landmarks or monuments are often the legacies and artefacts of profoundly resonant cultures that echo to this day. But they are not catalysts. Today they are far more likely to be signs of aspiration than achievement, and are no more likely to produce culture than tyre tracks would be to produce a car.

Cultural evolution has more in common with divination than design. A city can't build a culture any more than it can build an idea, a thought process or a polar bear. Cultures emerge from the spontaneous, temporary nature of human motivations, passions, interactions and enthusiasms. They often form in rebellion and opposition rather than by deliberation and design. They are unique and idiosyncratic. They result from adaptation and evolution, and they have a tendency to be strongest in the places where no one is looking or particularly wants them to be.

All is not lost. Once you let go of the idea that cultures are constructed, new possibilities emerge. Cultures can be nurtured. Cities can seed and feed culture. They can give it somewhere to live, to move, to breed, to grow. And when it fails (as it often does), they can provide fertile ground to go to seed in. Cultures are living things – they die as often from ill-thought-out initiatives to preserve, protect or resuscitate them as they do from starvation. They live in a complex ecosystem of regulation, regeneration, tax laws, economic decline and resurgence, subsidy, anarchy, inspiration, history, technology and – most importantly of all – the unpredictable, unquantifiable and subjective fertiliser of human creativity.

Great cultural cities are those which allow their cultures to flow rather than freeze.

*

I grew up in a city engaged in a long, slow debate about what its culture was or should be. Newcastle, Australia is hardly a world-renowned cultural centre. But it is a place fortunate enough to be blessed with a strong sense of its unique identity. Economics, some distinctive geographical impediments and some unique challenges conspire to make the city anything but complacent about its place in the world.

Blessed only with the advantage of not being Sydney, Newcastle is Australia's second-oldest and seventh-largest city. For decades, Newcastle has been engaged in a long and ultimately losing fight for the title of Australia's largest non-capital city – now the Gold Coast. While both cities are blessed with great beaches, they are cities with very different histories and mythologies. One is an iconic, international, fast-growing by-word for a leisure lifestyle; the other contents itself with a gritty local pride that occasionally manifests itself in shouting down or knocking the teeth out of anyone who'd dare suggest the place is anything less than paradise on earth.

Newcastle is gradually emerging from a prolonged period of economic decline and recession. Once home to Australia's largest steelworks, a now non-existent shipbuilding industry and a hub for manufacturing and medium industry of the kind that Australia doesn't do anymore, Newcastle has been forced to confront its own economic mortality. By my late teenage years, in the early '90s, the unemployment rate was well into double figures and youth unemployment peaked above 40 per cent. Even a booming port and coal industry have been unable to bring life back to Newcastle's long and broken CBD. At last count there were still over a hundred empty shops on the two main streets. Hundreds more empty offices and vacant floors sit above them. Newcastle's entire mid-twentieth century CBD lies fractured by an earthquake and a rapidly changing world.

Growing up, no one would have suggested that Newcastle really had much of a culture. Culture was something that happened somewhere else. Culture was something that other people did. It was mostly something that had already happened. Great dead men and young Americans invented culture. Culture was imported. It was filtered by experts and occasionally brought to the Civic Theatre by the likes of the Sydney Theatre Company, the Sydney Symphony Orchestra and big-name artists from far-flung places in Australia and overseas. The closest Newcastle really came to producing culture of any kind was when the Bell Shakespeare Company (led by local boy made good John Bell) would preview work in Newcastle before it got a run in Sydney. Whether this was practicality, nostalgia or because Novocastrians were discerning critics of Shakespeare (or not) was never entirely clear. But school kids got cheap enough tickets that I could afford to go.

As Newcastle sought its post-industrial roadmap, the idea of culture began to figure prominently in it. Cultural tourism, smarter jobs, innovation and the idea of a creative renaissance started to take hold. The Civic Theatre was immaculately and beautifully restored, cutting-edge architects were invited to redevelop the art gallery, massive old rail sheds were repaired and restored with the intent of turning them to cultural purposes, plans boldly proclaimed a large swathe of the CBD a 'cultural precinct,' the city's marketing material started to talk about Newcastle as a cultural centre and international consultants were brought in to talk about the rejuvenation of places like Dublin, Liverpool and Manchester.

Millions of dollars were spent. Many millions more were fantasised about or sought for projects that will never see the light of day. Yet the idea that Newcastle actually produced original culture was an afterthought. I did alright personally: some festivals I started brought artists and considerable audiences (fulfilling the tourism side of the equation), but the local creative community as a whole gained little.

In hindsight, cavernous heritage-listed buildings where trains were once built were ill-suited to the needs of artists. Their heritage status required infinite layers of planning permits and exemptions for every nail or partition, for every heavy object you might wish to drag across the floor. Government control meant activities were regulated to death and the entire place was schizophrenically required to convert to a function centre whenever a higher bidder demanded it.

A redeveloped art gallery, while desirable, was a long way down the list of potential creative catalysts. Though more impressive and less ugly than its predecessor, it wasn't much better for local artists than the current one. In any event, to date it has never happened.

Even the Civic Theatre's grand makeover was something of a mixed blessing. While the space was immaculately restored to accommodate major touring companies, its sheer scale meant that it was out of the reach of the innovative and adventurous, the local and low budget. The unglamorous and barely functional smaller theatre alongside it was not part of the renovation. It was quietly closed. It had not been kept up to date with ever-tightening Occupational Health and Safety requirements – a situation that remained until comparatively recently.

Drawings dotted with precincts marked 'cultural use'

remained plans. Practical attempts to kick-start or bootstrap cultural innovation were thwarted by increasingly complex regulations and requirements, tax breaks that created incentives for buildings to remain empty and an attitude that thwarted initiative and deterred all but the most belligerently persistent.

A decade later, Newcastle remains a net exporter of artists and a net importer of culture.

*

Newcastle is actually pursuing a pragmatic approach to cultural development. Cities awash with petro-dollars, status anxiety or a novelty-driven approach to economic development have turned to museums in the same way an earlier generation turned to theme parks. Abu Dhabi alone is spending billions to build both a Guggenheim and a Louvre. Cities the world over are allocating public funds to grand art museums to boost their economies by raising cultural status. Designed by brand-name celebrity architects, the world's major museums are slowly creating Disney-meets-Prada lifestyle brands.

By doing this, cities keen to project dynamism and confidence instead flout their insecurity. Cultural cringe is alive and well in the cities of the Middle East and East Asia. They look longingly to European palaces, monuments and art collections for cultural signs to clone. It is one of the ironies of the age that authoritarian states collect and celebrate the artefacts of Western rebellion, decadence, liberalism, tolerance, religiosity, conquest and conflict with almost no comment on the irony of it.

The brand-name museum competition is driven less by authentic local culture or the needs and aspirations of a city's artists or citizens, and more by the commercial instinct that drives a bid for a grand prix, Olympic Games or the world's tallest building.

No one suggests that a grand prix boosts the local automotive industry or a mega skyscraper is about office space. Sporting events are sold as tourism; only a fraction of the recurrent expenditure is passed off as investment in grass-roots sport.

For cities not awash in ludicrous sums of money, another template has emerged. Growth centres like Brisbane, Singapore and my adopted home of Melbourne chose from a common cultural menu: an 'iconic' (if not brand name) gallery, museum or performance centre, a 'flagship' art or film festival (ideally both), bringing great work from around the world, a 'world-class' theatre and/or dance company and/or orchestra that can present the greatest hits of Western culture. The relative size of these offerings is mistaken for the vibrancy or otherwise of a city's cultural life.

I have no objection to any of these. I've directed arts festivals, attended film festivals, and am partial to live performance. I love ambitious architecture, and regularly visit galleries at home and away. But I reject what they implicitly suggest about the cities that build and promote these limited set-piece choices. More often than not, they represent the same assumptions I grew up with in Newcastle: culture happens somewhere else; it is something a professional elite does for you; it is something that has already been created and a world city must archive it, present it and freeze it. Culture, as defined by a narrow model, is in need of constant investment, authorisation, attention and the intervention of a small army of bureaucrats, curators, professionals and middle managers who protect and sustain it.

Our arts agencies and governments spend much more money on this archival culture than on living culture. A single gallery can receive hundreds of millions of dollars of capital investment, over $40 million a year in government subsidies (with half spent on wages and a third on promotion), while artists in most Australian states compete for a collective pie of less than a million dollars to develop and present original work.

*

I'm a daydreamer. I love the idea of designing cities.

As a child, I drew maps of places that never existed. My shelves are full of books of architecture and urbanism. I've sketched ill-thought-out ideas and made sandbox cities to resemble the ones that I live in. I love the intricacies of how cities grow, evolve and change. I am part frustrated architect, part an under-capitalised property developer, part a great town planner of fictional utopias, and part the most petty of petty dictators.

I've played hours of Sim City – a computer game where the player assumes the role of all-powerful mayor and urban planner. I've patiently and gently tweaked land zonings and densities to make imaginary metropolises or boutique utopias and when that hasn't quite created the cities of my dreams, I've gone to the internet for cheat codes, downloaded the architecture and plonked a whopping big Guggenheim Bilbao right in that awkward spot that wasn't doing it for me.

In the real world, cultural institutions are the last place left where politicians and bureaucrats can play the central planning game. The last remnants of the grand 'nation-building' exercises of the black and white era. A throwback to a time when you might determine a public good, marshal massive state investments, and damn the years of recurrent funding and freeze a vision, an aspiration, and hold it out to the world.

Even conservatives of the kind who elevate competition and small government into a self-evident truth are often to be found among the most passionate advocates for this particular kind of cultural nation-building, subsidy and protectionism. Their passion for large, centralised, hierarchical cultural forms and approaches somehow overrides their ideological objection to large, centralised, bureaucratic hierarchies. They get outraged not by the day-to-day protectionism, but by when the walls are breached and someone actually creeps into the palace or on to the program with something that initially found its relevance in the competitive world outside.

My imaginary cities have people in them, but mostly they are there to stare at the awesome buildings and admire the ingenious planning. In reality, the ambitious scale dwarfs the idea that people might make culture in them. It draws to mind images of Adolf Hitler and Albert Speer standing over the massive model for their new world capital. Welthauptstadt Germania – with its grandiose edifices, sweeping boulevards and utter disregard of the human-scale consequences – was to be the fixed and immutable capital of the thousand-year reich. It is a vision of culture almost without people in it at all. It's a great irony that one of Hitler's last legacies is found in the city it was designed to replace. The anarchic, vibrant, culturally rich, robust and chaotic allure of post-reunification Berlin is alive to fluid possibility. It is the antithesis of his imagined city. Welthauptstadt Germania would have been fixed, grand, ambitious and barren.

I suspect the appeal of the grand institutions is as much to the desire in all of us to leave a legacy as it is to a rational and grounded response to the needs of culture. As the Sydney Opera House shows us, soaring ambitions create great narratives and compelling legacies for those who envisage, design and plan such an institution.. They leave fabulous legacies for those who open it and have their name on the plaque. They create jobs for those employed to run it and validate it and publicise it, do its paperwork and write reassuring reports that it has met its performance targets. They freeze culture long enough to quantify it.

Yet they ultimately mislead us into believing that culture is permanent and fixed, that culture stands steadfast against time and history. They lead us to believe that culture actually lives in buildings designed to stand for the ages. Yet, to all intents and purposes it dies there. The great arts are laid to rest and are archived there. So much energy and money are spent attempting to fossilise cultures that we have entirely forgotten to farm them.

Great cities are places where cultures are born, not their graveyards. A city is a unique set of possibilities. A city is a unique collision of ideas, catalysts for cultures to breed for people meet and interact, where possibilities are nurtured and integrated.

The truly great culture-producing cities may not have grand institutions. The art and cultural innovation they foster are more likely to emerge from the edges, not the centre.

*

Cultural planners may be best not to play too much Sim City. To really model the culture of cities, you would probably need a very different game where the city is not viewed as zones and grids, but as a series of tasks to be completed at street level – tasks such as finding somewhere to play, somewhere to rehearse, somewhere to exhibit, hang out and discuss with relatively limited capital. Finding somewhere to make mess and make noise. Somewhere to sell your work or somewhere that has enough flexibility that you can afford not to. Finding somewhere affordable and available at short notice, not bureaucratised and regulated to the point where your limited resources disappear before you have a chance to make the work or stage the production. Finding somewhere cheap enough to socialise and embrace or argue about ideas, even if you can't afford to pay for lunch and don't want to play the poker machines. Finding somewhere just far enough off the map to allow for experimentation, but close enough to others so you can get enough feedback to ensure that mistakes aren't perpetually repeated.

Cities look very different from street level than they do from the models of politicians, planners, dictators and computer game players. Culture looks very different from the point of view of the people making it than from the places where it is collected. Very few of the makers would prioritise grand palaces to their work, and even fewer will actually get into them. Artists in my experience generally want the reverse – they want to be able to take risks in places that are appropriate to take them in.

Artists need infrastructure that is fluid. They need places that are adaptable, accessible, breakable, spontaneous, flexible and capable of evolving quickly with their needs. They need spaces that are cheap, and more often they are willing to take all that goes with that and pay their own price in lack of facilities, endless working bees and leaky windows to compensate for it. Creative cities can build all the monuments they like, but accessibility rather than grandiosity is the key to living cultures.

Most cultural innovators and entrepreneurs don't need thousand-seat theatres. They don't need massive financial subsidies. They may fantasise about them, but their immediate concerns are generally much more basic. They need economic models that capitalise on their strengths and limit their weaknesses. While government grants and subsidies are vital and rarely refused, they're actually a second- or third-order issue in many cases – for anyone outside the world of recurrent funding grants, they are a way of solving practical problems rather than a source of income. Much more mundane questions like whether you can afford insurance, the availability of appropriate venues, whether you can have a bar and who gets to make money out of it are as profoundly important cultural questions as any philosophical aspirations.

In my experience, most artistic endeavours, from bands to exhibitions to theatre companies, short films, websites, festivals, conferences and installations, begin life as the results of pooled funds, sweat equity and very little cash. The ratio of things that creators can provide in kind (primarily labour, skill, sweat and enthusiasm) to the fixed costs that they cannot avoid is probably the major question that propels or thwarts cultural initiative.

The tangled minefield that stretches from public liability insurance to risk assessments, to liquor licensing, legal costs, copyright compliance, noise regulations, place of public entertainment licensing, is a formidable barrier to creative initiative. Collectively, these issues have been known to consume the resources of even a professional arts company and kill a not yet professional one much more quickly than a bad show. Obligatory consultants, large fees and the threat of heavy fines have clipped a lot of cultural activity before it ever started. Without a personal willingness to act responsibly but not necessarily thoroughly (or legally) in the face of these questions, I would never have got started. Culture is not so much what you plan but what you get away with.

The single largest area of expenditure for most small-scale cultural activities constitutes fees, insurance, infrastructure and reporting requirements that are either paid directly to government or as a result of a government requirement. For companies that are funded enough to cover those, the highest costs are most likely the administrative wages – with much of the bill spent on the additional cost of servicing government funding and meeting reporting requirements. Resourcing culture becomes little more than resourcing regulation. It is the norm in Australia for arts organisations to turn over hundreds of thousands of dollars and yet leave the artists themselves unpaid or barely paid. Very few companies in Australia would be in a position where the costs of artists, their tools and materials and the direct costs of putting on their work exceed their compliance and administration costs.

If cultures are fluid, each of these impediments is a dam wall that stops a fluid, living culture in its tracks.

*

Cities wishing to step ahead of the pack need to think beyond simply copying the 'world's best practice' cultural template. Cultural planning needs to think less in terms of hard infrastructure and subsidised companies and much more in terms of fluid communities and constantly changing opportunities. Beyond iconic buildings, flagship events and world-class companies lies an entire creative ecosystem largely ignored and an opportunity to foster a culture of creativity and not simply layers of bureaucracy.

The two models aren't mutually exclusive, but the reality is that the most efficient allocation of resources is to be found by brokering artists and creative communities with opportunities. Cities should find ways for artists and creative communities to invest their sweat equity in making and remaking their cultural infrastructure – be it temporary, commercial or publicly owned. It's cheaper, easier and allows for the kind of evolving and redefining that keeps cultures fluid as needs change.

In international cities, this is achieved through tax incentives for artists to use vacant or transitional buildings. In Australia, it is stifled by the tax deductibility of loss-making buildings and the fear of liability. More than anything, it is stifled by lack of prioritisation, direction and imagination.

Cities should embrace transition and transience, and let go of the idea that cultures are fixed. I come from an entire city in transition, but even the most prosperous Australian cities are full of empty blocks, vacant buildings and under-utilised government sites that have reached the end of their economic life. Their very transience provides unique opportunities that would never be possible in a glossy arts centre.

In virtually every suburb in Australia, there is a building that has been boarded up for years, while its permanent use is debated or deferred or a consultant is brought in to determine just how much it would cost to fix. Each passing day is a lost opportunity for a temporary art gallery, for a business to incubate, for a community to form, for a performance space, for a meeting point for social or cultural experimentation.

But cities also need permanent infrastructure of the practical kind. Cities need continuing places to play, to exhibit, to sell, to perform in, and around which to develop lasting and ongoing communities and audiences. Traditionally, government has only taken responsibility for these by owning them – either top-end institutions or community centres. In between, they have left all the other layers of informal infrastructure to the market – and the market in many places has failed. The reality is that we build our cities driven largely by commercial formulas and we subsidise our culture. In between, we have no mechanism or strategy to stimulate niche uses that may be profitable but not obscenely profitable. In New South Wales, with its obscene convergence of poker machines, political donations, property developers and a culture of conservative risk management, this has meant there are few remaining pubs used as live performance spaces. A flagrant disregard for community and cultural consequences has led to buildings, cities, suburbs and communities that are ludicrously profitable and culturally barren. A city requires the niche and the experimental, the commercial and profitable, the grand and the worthy, and as wide as possible a variety of the things in between.

To reach them, planning for culture needs to break out of the old paradigms of infrastructure, capital and subsidy, and to begin to look at the subtleties of cultural opportunities that the community itself might provide if the opportunities were encouraged.

*

Newcastle isn't where it used to be. Even since my own childhood the geographical isolation has changed. That Newcastle felt as far from the cultured world as was possible to be in an English-speaking country. But no city – even Newcastle – is truly and entirely on the edge anymore. Whereas once most media and most transportation came via Sydney, today

Newcastle plugs into a hundred channels and cheap daily flights to Brisbane, Sydney and Melbourne. The people of Newcastle are plugged into hundreds of thousands of global conversations – on blogs, websites, forums, mailing lists and bulletin boards. Newcastle exports a little culture now, and speaks directly with culture makers. Novocastrians post their photos, share bands they have seen, the events they have attended across networks of parallel global communities.

Newcastle's cultural connections are no longer scholarships, study tours, sabbaticals, reciprocal exhibitions or the passive receipt of culture broadcast from the great cultural centres of the world. Newcastle connects via the spontaneous, organic interactions that take place weekly, daily and hourly. Local artists and musicians have global communities with like minded people around the world.

Newcastle is part of the fluid forces of global cultural exchange – not as the top of a global pyramid but as part of a network of point-to-point cultural connections. Its cultural significance is measured less against whether it impresses Sydney, Melbourne, London or New York than who it connects directly to. Whether it prospers culturally will not be measured by purely by international art and style magazines, but by whether it is a hub or just a spoke, a consumer or a producer, an innovator or an afterthought in the global cultural milieu. That is a far more vital cultural measure than whether you have a landmark museum and a collection of Old Masters.

In a world made up of thousands of diverse subcultures or niche cultures, it is madness for a city to aspire to be just like other cities. Cities need places to celebrate the nature of culture that we have now. They need places where people uploading videos to YouTube can meet each other, and venues small enough to cater for the new diversity of contemporary music scenes. They need bars, galleries and performance spaces designed to capture the new paradox of communication: local work of international significance and international work of local significance.

Cities must trade in cultural cringe for a growing sense of confidence in our distinctiveness. They must try to be somewhere, not anywhere in the extended global sprawl of electronic suburbia. Cities must wilfully believe that the unique combination of events that may fuse here is just as compelling as those that may fuse somewhere else. Cities need to involve their people in making and remaking their own mythology, and create something that is truly unique.

Cities the world over need to contemplate the impossible long enough to see the possibilities emerge.

Originally published in *Griffith REVIEW Edition 20: Cities on the Edge*, May 2008.

BIBLIOGRAPHY

'A landlord's story: GPT', Empty Spaces Project, *University of Technology*, Sydney, 2010

Bellaiche, Jean-Marc, Chassaing, Thierry, and Kapadia, Sunil, 'Digital's disruption of consumer goods and retail', *BCG Perspectives*, The Boston Consulting Group, 2012

Belza, Jan, Forth, Patrick, Purnell, James, and Zwillenberg, Paul, 'Culture Boom. How digital media are invigorating Australia, *The Boston Consulting Group*, March 2012

Benfield, Kaid, 'The Death – and Life – of Small Downtown America', *The Atlantic Cities*, 7 September 2012

Bishop, Jen, 'Etsy CEO on using the marketplace to go global', *Dynamic Business*, 24 July 2012

Dagwell, Todd, 'Lonely Planet rates Newcastle in world's top 10', *Newcastle Herald*, 31 October 2010

De Lore, Amy, 'Rejuvenated mall the perfect Christmas gift', *Newcastle Herald*, 11 December 2009

'Diversification of the Hunter Economy – Post BHP', *The Hunter Valley Research Foundation*, 2011

'Economic Evaluation of 'Renew' Projects', Renew Newcastle, *SGS Economics and Planning*, December 2011

Excerpt from Marcus Westbury interview with *1233 ABC Newcastle*. Permission to quote courtesy of the ABC.

Farquhar, Liz, 'Jeff McCloy resigns as Newcastle Mayor over ICAC probe into Liberal Party banned donations scandal', *ABC News*, 18 August 2014

Fox, Justin, 'Why are commercial real estate markets so often gridlocked?, *Time*, 28 August 2009

Goldberg, Adrian, 'Businesses cut deals with charities to reduce tax bills', *BBC News*, 25 January 2012

Greenblat, Eli, 'What's killing off retailing?', *The Age, Business Day,* 7 September 2013

Hudson, Kris & O'Connell, Vanessa, 'Recession Turns Malls Into Ghost Towns', *The Wall Street Journal*, 1 May 2009

Judd, Nick, 'DIY Urban Development: Step One is to Start a Facebook Group', *Tech President*, 7 February 2011

'LGA Profile – Newcastle', Destination NSW, 2014

'Lonely Planet's top 10 cities for 2011', *Lonely Planet,* 31 October 2010

McGowan, Michael, 'Zac Zavos: From minor to roaring success', *Newcastle Herald*, 8 August 2014

Murphy Kelly, Samantha, 'Why 90% of Startups Fail', *Mashable*, 5 February 2013

'Newcastle's heritage', The City of Newcastle, http://www.newcastle.nsw.gov.au/about_newcastle/history_and_heritage/newcastles_heritage

'Newcastle Visitor Profile and Satisfaction Report', Summary of Results, *Tourism Research Australia*, October 2013

'Nook Store. Australian independent streetwear men's fashion', *HUNTERhunter,* 2015

NSW Retail Tenant's Guide, *Small Business Commissioner NSW,* 2005

Page, Donna, 'Rapid increase in empty shops in Newcastle CBD', *Newcastle Herald*, 29 November 2009

Poulter, Sean, 'High streets 'are losing 20 shops a day' as retail bloodbath turns many areas into ghost towns', *Daily Mail*, 1 March 2013

Pryor, Lisa, 'Coast with the most – why an old coal town could become our Berlin', *Sydney Morning Herald*, 13 September 2008. Permission to quote courtesy of the author.

Ralph Snowball archives, courtesy of University of Newcastle: https://www.flickr.com/photos/uon/sets/with/72157608912691810

Richards, Edwina, 'Renew Newcastle Case Studies: Make Space and Studio Melt'. Permission to quote courtesy of the author.

Salmon, Felix, 'Empty storefronts', *Reuters*, 31 August 2009

Sterling, Bruce, 'Renew Newcastle', *Wired*, 12 July 2009

Taffel, Jacqui, 'Regional artists find new ways to sell their wares', *Sydney Morning Herald*, 21 September 2013

Urban Growth NSW, 'Newcastle – East End – Overview', *Urban Growth NSW,* http://www.urbangrowthnsw.com.au/work/urban-transformation-projects/newcastle-east-end.aspx

Whitely, Patrick, 'The era of prosperity is upon us', *China Daily*, 19 October 2007

'Who's Gone Bust in Retailing 2010-12?', *Centre for Retail Research*, August 2012

'Work in Selected Culture and Leisure Activities, Australia, Apr 2007', *Australian Bureau of Statistics*, Released 19 December 2007

Yglesias, Matthew, 'Gentrificationphobia', *Slate*, 8 October 2012
Yglesias, Matthew, 'Licensed to Decorate', *Slate*, 20 May 2012

Marcus Westbury is an accidental urbanist, consultant, speaker, writer and broadcaster and the founder of Renew Newcastle and Renew Australia. He is based in Melbourne, Australia. He may even be available to speak, consult or collaborate on interesting projects. You can email him at marcus@marcuswestbury.net

www.creatingcities.net
Includes images, background and additional information about this book.

www.renewnewcastle.org
For a full history of current and former Renew Newcastle projects

www.marcuswestbury.net
For blog posts, updates and general links.

Printed in Australia
AUOC02n0324100717
287434AU00001B/1/P

9 780992 568740